FORGOTTEN MANUSCRIPT

First published by Charco Press 2023
Charco Press Ltd., Office 59, 44-46 Morningside Road, Edinburgh
EH10 4BF

Work published with funding from the 'Sur' Translation Support Programme
of the Ministry of Foreign Affairs of Argentina / Obra editada en el marco
del Programa 'Sur' de Apoyo a las Traducciones del Ministerio de Relaciones
Exteriores y Culto de la República Argentina.

A CIP catalogue record for this book is available from the British Library.

ISBN: 9781913867713
e-book: 9781913867720

www.charcopress.com

Edited by Fionn Petch
Cover designed by Pablo Font
Typeset by Laura Jones
Proofread by Carolina Orloff

MIX
Paper from
responsible sources
FSC
www.fsc.org   FSC® C013056

Sergio Chejfec

FORGOTTEN MANUSCRIPT

Translated by
Jeffrey Lawrence

CHARCO PRESS

TRANSLATOR'S NOTE

Sergio Chejfec and I worked closely together on *Forgotten Manuscript*. He first approached me about translating the book in early 2019, and over the next few years, we discussed it regularly by email, in person, and over Zoom. At the time of Sergio's passing in April 2022, I had completed a full draft of the translation, with his input on decisions regarding its content and style. I'm deeply sorry that Sergio is not here to see *Forgotten Manuscript* in its published form. But I'm consoled by the fact that readers in English now have access to this extraordinary work, a testament to a life that was dedicated to writing and to thinking about what writing means.

Jeffrey Lawrence
October 1, 2022

*Our writing equipment takes part
in the forming of our thoughts.*
Friedrich Nietzsche

O_ne._ This book can be read as the story of a notebook. One could call it a journal or a composition book – it doesn't really matter – the important thing is that I've had it with me for a great deal of time.[1] I adopted it immediately when I laid eyes on it, half-forgotten in the display window of an inconspicuous shop in a far-flung neighbourhood of a city that I barely knew and where I had wandered for lack of anything better to do.

The scene was the following: a series of long, neutral streets that sparked neither curiosity nor enthusiasm. In the middle of the empty morning, a brisk morning, someone stopped before the store window of a small shop. I was that someone, looking intently at the green

---

1   Or it can be read as the effects of the notebook's presence over a number of years. Anything present for long enough begins to haunt one. Generally speaking, I don't like it when objects speak or make arguments for me. The notebook will therefore be present in these pages even though I mention it infrequently; it is the remote inspiration or hazy backdrop for many of these reflections on writing. Apropos of Nietzsche's quote: the notebook is not an instrument I use to write and then think, and then write again when I'm so inclined (that is, an artifact that adapts itself to each situation), but rather an accessory I carry with me to remind myself of the strangeness of writing, the eternal flame that, paradoxically, is not always visible. The notebook is an amulet, but also an article of faith. Moreover, it's the sign of my personal belief, which is also shared by many others: the belief in the written word. Could anyone possibly believe that writing doesn't exist? It would be like denying the existence of rain. The notebook has thus come to represent the various links to writing that find support in my changing attitudes toward that belief.

notebook next to a slim, similarly-hued vase that could barely fit two flowers. Perhaps it was the curious visual composition wrought by the two objects that initially caught my attention: the thick notebook like the squat and sturdy foundations of a factory; the vase a towering chimney from whose heights the ovens hidden within the building (the notebook) released their slender columns of heat and ash. It was as if in the midst of that redoubled solitude – the solitude of the store window and the solitude of the street – these two beings (if I may call them that) had been ushered into a silent and distant exile akin to the space of a museum.

I immediately became attached to that notebook. In the first place, I was drawn to the fact that it was a rustic object, lacking in any sort of sophistication or elegance. Second, it was incredibly cheap. Later I learned it was made in China. At that time, Chinese products had not yet colonized the world as completely as they later would – and I like to think that the successful assault of those flawless notebooks paved the way for the later conquest; the relatively successful assault, I should say, because I have never come across a notebook like that again.

The Origin of the 'Problem'

The notebook has been with me since that day, a day when I was just wandering around and of which I nevertheless have the most vivid, enduring memories. Memories, for instance, of the urban landscape: blocks and blocks of nondescript buildings and empty lots that one could cross diagonally to reach the adjacent streets. Or rather, broad, inviting shortcuts that allowed anyone with a modicum of spatial awareness to save time, as if the street grid itself were optional.

That afternoon I failed to notice one practical aspect about the notebook: its sheer number of pages, approximately three hundred. All white in colour, though time would turn them yellow, each with twenty-two lines, a hypnotic regularity. It evoked a calm sea about to be traversed, or an endless horizontal plane, page after page.[2] Its thickness made it even more singular: it wasn't one of those notebooks that one uses and then quickly throws away. Here's an image of it, both in its closed and open state:

Cover and blank pages of the green notebook

Out on the street once more, I felt utterly pleased with myself considering the enormous step I had taken towards the organization, or better yet the unification, of my notes. Up to that point I had jotted things down on loose pages, sheets folded in half or ripped from notepads, once I had fully articulated a note or thought. The Chinese notebook moved me to gather these observations into a single place, though I should make clear

2 A memory: the wonder that lined pages produced in me when I first began to write. I vividly recall my shame at the impatience of my first-grade teacher after I raised my hand, while all of the other students were calmly bent over their desks, and asked if I could keep writing once the lines had ended.

that I wasn't drawn to its utilitarian qualities – which certainly might appeal to someone else – but rather its fragile appearance, which, as I say, induced in me an immediate pact of cohabitation.

The notebook was also a sign of the imminent (or perhaps already existent; in any case I was unaware of it) proliferation of small notebooks and journals of various brands and designs (first and foremost the Moleskine); during this same period, I began to receive a series of stylish writing journals – as if the green notebook in my possession had opened the floodgates. They were the perfect gift for anyone who identified as a writer. I remained faithful to the Chinese notebook even as the other notebooks piled up, though given my own writing habits this led to serious difficulties and certain associated fears – difficulties and fears that have stayed with me through the years, as I will now explain.

For me the notebook represents a kind of problem. It is a cherished object from which I will never part (the few times I thought I lost it I felt something akin to a physical threat; as if an essential part of my being were at stake), and yet it is also something that, when I write in it from time to time, seems highly unstable, so much so that it occasionally slips from my memory as if it were made of an evanescent material, or as if it simply didn't belong to me in the same form in which it exists in the world. Does this mean that the things we cherish most are the things that are most indeterminate?

Two. At a certain moment in my shifting relationship to the notebook, and perhaps because of it, I discovered the anomaly encrypted in the eloquent yet unstable presence of the written word. Something that allowed me insight into a dimension of writing by hand that had escaped me up until that point. I'm not referring to my own reasons for writing — those have always been clear — but rather the physical act of composition itself. I had developed an erratic relationship to my manually written notes. One of my greatest and most recurrent fears was (and still is) that I would never fill those three hundred pages.

I write this in the past tense, but the truth is that I'm also referring to the present. The idea that I would never fill the notebook seemed more likely than the idea that I would. It was a Sisyphean scenario. It meant forever renouncing the desire to adopt a new notebook (and consequently renouncing the desire to relive the anarchic joy of starting afresh with clean pages). But it also meant something else that it took more time for me to comprehend, paradoxically because it was such a simple fact: filling the notebook's pages could be interpreted as having completed a piece of writing. It was similar, in other words, to *finishing* — or better yet *having* — a book. One of those acts that acquires its true meaning precisely because it is borrowed from something else: in this case, from the idea of publication. Due to this numerical similarity between the notebook's pages and the pages of a published book, my writing thus revealed itself to me as an inadvertent simulation — I was unprepared for this altered format, however, because of my somewhat accidental relationship to the process of writing by hand.

All signs indicated that the notebook would remain unpublished. This reminded me in turn of another kind of illusion. When I was first becoming a writer, I built up an enormous reserve of patience (or impatience?) regarding the publishing process in general, and publishing houses more particularly. Elsewhere I have referred to the problem of having a notebook filled with endless observations: as time passes, one feels that the notebook becomes the evidence of what one has failed to write rather than what one has already written. In this instance, I thought that in terms of posterity – whatever that means – what would remain was an incomplete notebook, the sign of a sort of textual indolence on the part of the so-called author, who was incapable of filling up a small number of pages given the many opportunities he was given to progress over several long decades.

And so the green notebook accompanies me almost like a mistaken talisman. An object that shames and inhibits me. It reminds me of what I'm not, and thereby affirms what I am. It makes me believe, though nothing else in reality corroborates this, that everything I do is in an embryonic stage. That I'm always stopping and starting my writing in the very same motion.[3]

---

3 I believe this ambivalence derives from my unnatural relationship to literature, and in particular to writing. Not long ago, I participated in a public interview with a well-known writer. With such writers, I believe that one should never ask direct questions. One should surround them with thoughts related to their texts, texts that are largely known to the world by the ideas contained within them. One of the things that I thought to say, but in the end couldn't find the opportunity to point out – it's not difficult to see why – is the following: writers can be divided into two camps, those who have a natural relationship to literature and those who don't. I don't mean that a natural relationship implies a peaceful relationship, or vice versa, that a non-natural relationship implies a conflicted one. Rather, I believe that some writers adopt from the outset a proximity to literature, while others approach it through all sorts of stratagems and hesitations. In Argentina, the archetype, as always, is Borges. The very self-construction of his figure shows him surrounded by books, reading from an early age more naturally than if he were speaking. I'm reminded here of Arturo Carrera's metaphor, when he refers, in his work with Alfredo Prior, to 'children born with a hairstyle', but also of something else I once heard him say: *writers born with a hairstyle*. Graced with something more than simply knowledge: a kind of belonging or familiarity that goes hand in hand with their literary development. As if they had been born knowing they would be writers. At the other extreme, it's easy to identify writers who come to their literary

My ambivalent relationship to writing by hand, an act to which I feel infinitely devoted and which nevertheless lacks practical application, is at the root of some of the questions that this kind of writing, almost a ritual or ethnographic exercise, continues to inspire in me, and even more so of the intriguing yet evasive material that I continue to find in every detail that appears at each step of composition.

Three. The act of writing longhand extends through time in a unique way. It's as if such writing could go on forever. It's likely that the appeal of handwritten manuscripts derives from this assurance of continuity, which relies on a further (though mistaken) promise: that of immutability. Nevertheless, it also owes something to other modes of writing; all modes of writing draw their appeal from their mutual influences and complementary shortcomings. One is drawn toward handwritten manuscripts because, unlike more mediated forms of writing (whether produced by typewriters, word processors, or automatic transcription tools), they alone retain the signs of hesitation.[4]

---

connection as something unnatural, and construct that relationship through other means.

4   By hesitation I don't mean textual indecision (what word to use, how to continue a thought, etc.), or not only that, but also the vacillation inherent in every person's handwriting. Even in the most beautiful and measured scripts one can find these marks; it's a feature common to nearly all writers. One case that particularly interests me is that of Juan José Saer, to whom I will return later on. Years ago, when I had the chance to read his manuscripts, I found in some of them – though not all – a breakdown in every 's' that appeared in the middle of a word. As if each time he penned one he needed to rest, or had trouble connecting it to the next letter. I found that words that contain an 's' had a slightly larger space than normal, especially when that 's' was followed by a consonant. Those hesitations obsess me to

The starting point for the ideas that follow is my cohabitation with the aforementioned green notebook. A shared intimacy that poses more questions than those I have been able to formulate while writing in the blank pages themselves.

Forms of Imitation

The notebook is a handy object if I need an alternative to the computer. Its pages sometimes collect notes and sometimes a slightly different form of writing that corresponds to a story or essay that I'm writing. I also jot down more concrete information: places, names, instructions, ideas I want to remember. If I need to write something down quickly, for instance when someone calls, and I only have the notebook near me, it creates a dilemma, because I'm absolutely incapable of ripping out even the smallest piece of this well-worn but always available object.

Does this mean that the notebook is, at times, a substitute for the computer, that what I write in the former is a substitute for what I write in the latter? I don't think it's an easy comparison. In the first place, because the notebook is not a machine, and the computer is. As a machine, the computer can do many things – for example, act as one's proxy in destroying a text. What I mean is that if I see that a document or part of a document 'inside'

the point that, lacking a ready answer, I tend to look for an aesthetic or structural explanation, and I begin to make associations: for instance, between reflexivity (well established in the case of Saer, whose narrative form revolves around repetition) and the form of his script. These hypotheses don't go anywhere, but they help me to ascribe a purpose to handwritten manuscripts that is independent from the material traces they have left.

the computer isn't working, I have no problem deleting it. But I'm incapable of crossing out even a single word, phrase, or fragment in the notebook once I've written it down.

I don't know what this suggests. That my attachment to the notebook is greater than my attachment to my own writing? I also wonder if the almost devotional bond that ties me to the notebook arises from a negative or even spectral condition, since, when I pause for reflection, I recognize that the vertigo I experience when confronted by the void that its pages represent stems from everything I've written using other media and on other surfaces. The notebook's pages would thus represent the foundation of something that cannot be seen because it is written elsewhere; the free space that must be preserved precisely because it symbolizes a place of exchange, a quiet textual mass that lurks behind the whiteness, or simply a parallel dimension to that other domain in which the writing process is actually occurring.

There is a third way of thinking about this notebook, green on the outside and yellow on the inside. Sooner or later most of what I write there ends up being copied elsewhere. I like that it functions as a space of transition, and not just a secondary object for my writing, that what I put there necessitates a more or less indirect translation. In this way, despite my intermittent use of it (though with a habitual frequency), the notebook reveals its importance to me through two procedures that I associate with the idea of literary creation: writing by hand (even as I've almost entirely set it aside) and the act of transcription.[5]

---

5 Transcription is a task I readily associate with revision and rewriting; it is therefore almost inextricably linked to the idea of literary creation and conceptualization. Although with the advent of word processing programs transcription is no longer necessary, as it was for typewriters or longform manuscripts, it continues to operate mentally

Four. There was a time many years ago when I spent whole afternoons copying out Kafka's tales. I had some soft-cover brown notebooks – school notebooks, though with few pages. It wasn't just that they were formatted for students: I also thought that I would absorb something from the author through the act of transcription. Although I could detail now all the things I thought I absorbed, the most important one was a certain kind of feeling.

I found in his stories an inscrutable feeling that I didn't want to incorporate so much as to get to know. But there's no other way to get to know a feeling than to feel it yourself, even if it's just for a few seconds and mediated by the act of reading. I therefore surrendered to these copying sessions, in solemn silence and with a discipline that bordered on desperation. I hoped to produce a connection between the two feelings – Kafka's and mine – through the transcription of his stories – which, to make matters more complicated, were themselves translations into Spanish of the German originals.

Nevertheless, these exercises weren't just about copying. They also became a habit of reading, insofar as copying by hand came to signify for me an ideal kind of textual comprehension – one achieved at a particularly slow pace. One could describe the exercises as 'translations' only if that word is emptied of all meaning. How should I put it? They were reconstructive readings, toward which I employed the only intangible good I had at the time: my skill as a copyist.[6]

---

as the symbol of various processes of rewriting, progress, and textual development. Notably, the work of rewriting and transcribing allows one to produce 'originals' at the same time that, in paradoxical terms, one becomes further removed from them with each transcription or rewriting.

6 A 2007 film by Joao Moreira Salles, *Santiago*, also speaks of writing as a form of copying and appropriation. Though it may seem

In a subsequent phase I began to write stories or tales directly inspired by Kafka, perhaps because I believed that the transcription exercises had had a positive effect. I didn't focus on my own handwriting, since by now I was deeply proud of it. It was the perfect instrument for reliving my spiritual kinship with the great writer, which had previously been produced by the transcription, during which, of course, the quality of my handwriting

---

tangential to the plot, the protagonist's passion for transcribing finds an inverse reflection in the violation of the documentary ethos at the close of the film. The film is dedicated to Santiago Badariotti Merlo, the former butler for Moreira Salles' family. It can be seen at <youtu.be/SygdBiTCWEg>. At certain moments the film shows the transcriptions done by Santiago during various periods of his life. The scene presents his 'old machine-gun', a Remington typewriter (Friedrich Kittler refers in his book, which I will cite later on, to the prominent role that the great arms manufacturers played in the mass dissemination of typewriters; a fact that Julio Cortázar may very well have had in mind when he proposed the metaphor of the machine gun as the revolutionary substitute for the typewriter). In any case, Santiago Badariotti copied some thirty thousand book pages, on three continents and over the span of various decades. He had a preference for aristocracies and dynastic histories – from any country, region, or culture – particularly for great empires and powerful lineages. He stuck with the original languages of the books, which he transcribed scrupulously onto blank pages or hotel stationary. To the side of his favourite scenes he added enthusiastic or censorious comments. In the film there is a notable contrast between the emptiness of the great and now vacant Salles house and the abundance of Santiago's small apartment, overflowing with objects, decorations, and cultural relics. Santiago's legacy consists of these thirty thousand transcribed pages, which, arranged in stacks of thick paper, fill an entire bookcase. Papal histories, for instance, take up more than one thousand pages. The immense materiality of Santiago's undertaking requires a range of different writing techniques and implements, most of them 'amateurish'. Serious art might view his undertaking with admiration or with mistrust, but rarely with full understanding.

had been of the utmost importance.[7]

In those Kafkian stories, my primary difficulty was that I could not simply do away with commonplace actions and scenes (one could say that the same problem existed for Kafka, but he knew how to employ it in the service of his art). In Kafka everything sounded so mythic, yet the feelings expressed were so human that I thought the only way to absorb them was through some method of adapting them. (Perhaps somewhere else I will describe the strange sense of connection and divergence that I felt for a long time when reading Kafka's stories.)

The problem was that from the outset my 'adaptations' had that 'feeling' that I alone was in a position to understand. It actually consisted of abstract and circular variations on arbitrary themes, which I couldn't bear to abandon because they constituted the only element that could sustain my creative imagination. Everything else was either a direct allusion to Kafka's work or a depiction of petty resentments and parallelisms that were intended to be universal but that were in fact expressions of my own private code.

Those Kafkian notebooks – both the ones that contained the transcriptions of Kafka's stories and the ones that contained stories influenced by him – have now disappeared. As I mentioned, the notebooks had few pages, making them singularly appropriate for Kafka's dense and abbreviated parables. Yet I retain the memory of my faith in writing by hand: the essential instrument

---

7 I had acquired, as the former pupil of a vocational school, a style of handwriting known as handprinting (*imprenta manuscrita*), which is similar to the use of block letters (*letra de imprenta*), except that the latter is typically reserved for filling out forms, while the former refers to a habitual kind of handwriting. Basically, manual print consists of emulating the standard style of the typewriter, and it's created by clearly separating one letter from the next. It was considered a more legible style, particularly suited to diagrams, tables, equations, and reports.

thanks to which my feelings about writing coalesced, and through which the gifts heretofore forbidden to me were imitated, if not fully acquired. I also remember that this mechanical faith in writing by hand often led to an innocent and – let's say – textual euphoria that I am now only rarely able to recreate.

Perhaps this is why writing has always been linked to an idea of moral discipline for me – a discipline I have difficulty abandoning even now that I am closer to the end of my time writing than I am to the beginning. Kafka was my only model. I therefore needed to tap into his spiritual style at a deep level – that was what justified my writing; moreover, I needed to be conscious of the meaning and implications of what I was writing, as if the development of the narrative were not dissimilar to a profound and organized form of argumentation. Because the point was to etch a truth deep in the hidden structure of the story – not so deep, however, as to be unverifiable.

But I'm not writing this to talk about Kafka, whose writing practices have been discussed often enough. I will only note that for me it was through the practice of writing by hand, whether transcribing or copying, that I began to adopt other people's contents, feelings, and abilities. The act of composition, the shaping of the letters, the whole silent ceremony – everything was conducted according to protocols that came from elsewhere but that secretly offered me a hospitality that the outside world denied me. And from this arose another element: writing as something that must be performed. Performed so that it would reach an authentic degree of naturalness, so that every one of the poses, inclinations, and attitudes related to writing would be a more effective form of salvation, not so that I myself would change, but so that this additional naturalness related to writing and literature in general would save me from anxiety and loneliness.

It might sound naïve, but because of all this, writing continues to offer me various degrees of irreducible mystery. Of course, given everything I've just said, that mystery doesn't derive from my own practice. Rather, it emerges when, on occasions, I observe the effects or characteristics of the writing of others.

Five. Two works of installation art connected to creative writing. Although I don't see them as complementary projects – in fact, one might consider them to be somewhat opposed – I have the sense that they reflect an important dilemma about how to assimilate the sheer range of different material practices that have come to define writing in our contemporary moment, the distinct instruments and modalities through which the activity of writing takes place.

The material forms of writing are diverse, and they imply various kinds of devices; yet the paradox, at least for now, is that their results are relatively similar. The organization of text remains basically the same as it was in the past: word, line, paragraph, page. Only those experiences that either derive from or are proximate to hypertext have succeeded in destabilizing the measured progression expressed in the form of lineation and textual concatenation. And even in the case of hypertext this destabilization is limited: whenever the mass of text migrates away from the digital sphere, it must return to the enclosure of the page and the spatial hierarchies of the printed book.

The two installations I am referring to build on the ideas and practices of copying – copying in the writerly sense of the word. When one copies without using mechanical, chemical, or electronic means, one's only option is to replicate the writing: to literally transcribe the succession of words and signs that make up the text. It's the kind of artistic project that places manual labour – by which I mean the physical effort related to the aesthetic or conceptual proposition – in a recognizable position. Or to put it slightly differently, the material task is the sine qua non that determines the nature of the work of art, because without it the conceptual dimension would simply be reduced to the status of an idea, a reduction all too common in other cases. It's a physical reverie as well, insofar as it entails the exercise of a properly artistic skill whose virtuosity (or mere execution) seeks to compensate for the more conceptual aspects of the work. I refer to a work by Fabio Kacero and a series of performances by Tim Youd that later became artworks.

I didn't have the chance to see Kacero's installation, a handwritten version of Borges' famous story 'Pierre Menard, Author of the Quixote'.[8] My sense is that the idea of the copy performs a more physical than pictorial function in this work. Kacero eschews the option of a mere literal transcription (for which it would be enough to simply rewrite the text using any style of writing), but he also refuses to imitate Borges' own original manuscript (for which he would have had to take each page of the original as a precise combination of script, lines, slants, and slips, and where the thickness of the line, the specific type of paper, etc. would have been important factors). Instead, the purpose seems to have been to achieve the shape of each one of Borges' letters individually – perhaps as an ironic attempt to create

8   The installation was part of a Kacero retrospective, *Detournalia*, in the Museo de Arte Moderno de Buenos Aires from July 3 to October 19, 2014. At the time, I was far from Buenos Aires. I asked two friends to try to obtain an exhibition catalogue; one was told the catalogue was sold out, the other that it had never been printed due to a lack of funds. The latter friend, P, supportive of my curiosity, went to take pictures and videos of the show, which he later sent to me, though for obvious reasons those are difficult for me to reproduce in this book.

a sort of Borgesian typeface[9] – but at the expense of avoiding the writerly mark, that is, the true canvas of every writer: the manuscript as a plastic negotiation with and on the white surface of the page.

Fabio Kacero, two pages from *Fabio Kacero, autor de Jorge Luis Borges, autor de Pierre Menard, autor del Quijote.* 2006. Pen on A4-sized paper.

Kacero's graphological resolve results in a non-technical reproduction (i.e. not mediated by technology; perhaps we should call it an 'atechnical' reproduction) of Borges' handwriting. There is an effort at manual adaptation, let's say, and of calligraphic convergence. Kacero masters the author's script; he recreates it as if it were the inimitable stroke of an artist – which indeed

---

9   A sort of Borgesian Lorem ipsum? Maybe that's partially true, to the degree that the Borgesian, at whatever level we define it, has long since become a lingua franca through which different aesthetic forms and styles derive a kind of conceptual common meaning, with the guarantee of a certain level of critical sophistication.

it is.[10] In fact, the project also partakes of the oscillation or ambiguity that often exists between the notions of 'copy' and 'imitation'. If it's true that all handwriting is unique by nature, and to a greater or lesser degree rejects imitation as a form of fraud, the idea of the copy requires a prior form of validation. In this case it's the concept of the 'original', and the qualities that radiate from it – in other words Borges' handwriting as the mark of his authorship of his works – that makes Kacero's operation relevant rather than simply random.

Furthermore, the tension between the idea of the copy and the idea of imitation also hovers over Borges' story itself. The narrator wants us to believe that Menard has imitated Cervantes in such a unique and effective way that he has achieved the same literary result; at the same time, on another level, the story implies that what Menard has actually done is to 'copy' the Quixote, and that the genius that is attributed to him is really only the product of the narrator's own reading method. As if the story were saying: Menard was a genius if he imitated Cervantes, but not if he merely copied him.[11]

---

10   I exchanged some messages with Kacero about the installation as I was finishing this book. I will cite this sentence of his, which describes one of the lasting effects of the operation and some of its premises: '(…) once I decided to appropriate the story, it didn't seem to me that Borges' handwriting was necessary for the work. Nevertheless, I retained it. What's more, my own handwriting was never the same again. It became a kind of mix of Borges' and the handwriting I had prior to the work. A "successful fusion", as Brundle's machine informs us neutrally in Cronenberg's film *The Fly*, after developing the monstrous hybrid.' Fabio Kacero, 17 April 2015.

11   Of course, I'm simplifying the conceptual implications of Borges' Menard, especially those concerning the role of reading, which I don't elaborate on here so as not to confuse my point. From this perspective, 'Pierre Menard' may be among the least interesting

The original manuscript of 'Pierre Menard' has become an iconic stand-in for Borges' handwritten style, and also – of course – a philological document relating to the text itself (for those scholars who focus their study on changes, additions, and eliminations). Kacero's original borrows from Borges' original a notion of authority that it cleaves to excessively – at least at first glance – perhaps because it does not attempt to resolve the irresolvable tension between copy and imitation that the installation itself puts on display.

Six. Writing by hand has always been a powerful symbolic tool. In writers' origin stories we often find scenes of them enacting painstaking scriptive mimesis as a means of aesthetically, intellectually, or even morally appropriating their most revered and untouchable influences. This faith in the instantaneous pedagogical virtues of writerly imitation might be seen as evidence of an extremely impoverished painterly conception that writers tend to have about their own handwriting. The supreme importance they attribute to their written script derives from a belief external to the literary discipline properly speaking; it takes its model from the visual arts, where identifiable mark-making is crucial to the development of style and technique.

Nevertheless, writing is a major literary theme, in the sense that longhand writing is increasingly a key factual demonstration of self-reflexivity in a world slowly being emptied of such demonstrations. We might recall Mario Levrero's veritable leitmotif, when in *Empty Words* he subjects himself to exercises to change his handwriting as a method for improving his own moral character and the merits of his work. Or

of Borges' stories for a consideration of handwritten style, a topic that is more directly relevant to many of his other writings.

likewise the change that Robert Walser experienced when he gave up his pen (the object that he believed had annihilated him as a writer) and adopted a small pencil, which led him to new knowledge, a reinvigorated written script, and a lasting return to literature in the form of his well-known micrograms – all despite his mental instability. He himself claimed that changing his writing instrument increased his wellbeing.

Is it fair then to ask: what fantasy does Kacero's exercise on Borges' Menard play out? The appropriation of Borges himself or the appropriation of his method? Are these mutually exclusive possibilities? Perhaps it's a more obvious form of appropriation: the style of a written script detached from the paper that serves as its support, a sort of timeless treasure that drifts through the lingua franca of manuscript originals, using its immaterial condition to stay just above the surface.

I learned through a friend of a case of forged manuscripts perpetrated by a poet named G. One day my friend ran into G in Buenos Aires while the poet was scouring the city's used bookstores for old student notebooks. An American university had offered him money for the original manuscripts of his books, and since he didn't have any of the originals, or hadn't saved any, he was determined to recreate them meticulously, sparing no detail in their fabrication. Those supposedly timeworn originals eventually reached their destination, and are now being preserved as what they effectively are: handwritten manuscripts. The story reminds me of the backdated and artificially aged photographs that Man Ray (or someone in his circle) began to distribute when his inventory of early 'originals' ran out.

It's likely that the conceptual aspects of the Argentine poet's operation were adapted to his immediate needs. The whole episode strikes me as emblematic of how institutions ask artists for something they are able to provide, but whose cost is the relaxation of the notion of originality. Kacero also fabricated an original for exhibition in an institution; the difference between his case and the cases of G and Man Ray is that in this instance the fabrication was transparent: it was the very gesture of appropriation that certified the conceptual density of the work. Another way to say this is that the gesture of appropriation is precisely that which was forbidden to G and Man Ray. That is because, as I've already made clear, the act of appropriation always oscillates between being a virtue and a fraud. What Kacero needed to make explicit is exactly what G and Man Ray had to hide.

The idea of the original is different – and complex in a different way – in the case of Tim Youd. His project consists of 'retyping' approximately one hundred *important* works of literature. He makes use of first editions (the text he copies) and typewriters that are similar to the ones used by the authors in composing those works (this amounts to a substantial reduction in Youd's corpus, since the authors must have written the original on a typewriter). These writing performances typically last a few months and they are often carried out during the open hours of the places where they are staged, usually museums and libraries – institutions that have an inherently conflicted relationship to the ephemeral. Youd's sessions don't aim to break records for the length of time spent in front of the typewriter; they span a normal working day. As the artist's website informs, through the end of 2014 he had retyped between twenty and thirty novels.[12]

---

12 The author's website is www.timyoud.com. In November 2014, alongside other information, Youd announced his schedule of performances through mid-2015, including in many instances the model of typewriter he would use. For instance, in April of 2015,

To say that he is retyping these novels might seem confusing, but there's no other way to describe the process. It might seem confusing because we typically assume that retyping entails generating a legible written copy of the original, in the cumulative style of Santiago Badariotti, the butler of the Moreira Salles family. In my opinion, if this were Youd's practice we might see him as the kind of avenger who could unmask Menard: copying is nothing more than a mechanical gesture; a task more appropriate to those in conventional occupations such as notaries or scribes. (Another way to put it: in the world of art, one is either Duchamp or Menard; in the real world, one is Santiago Badariotti.)

But Youd does not generate a sequential body of text through his copying, basically because he does not change pages as he types. The result of every one of his performances is a diptych: a sheet of paper saturated with ink (usually black), since he has written the entire novel on a single page; and another sheet, behind the first, which has indentations produced by the typewriter's keys and ink stains in those areas where the marks on the first page bled through.

As a complement to this residually vocational work, Youd exhibits typewriters made from cardboard or light wood, copies of each respective model of typewriter used by Youd during his performances. The visitor to the exhibit will thus see the motley, illegible text of the transcription alongside a bastard copy of the instrument used to produce it.

Youd anticipated transcribing Virginia Woolf's *To the Lighthouse* with an Underwood Universal.

Tim Youd, *Black Spring, by Henry Miller*, 201 pages typed on an Underwood Standard. Tim Youd: Los Angeles, April 2013

Tim Youd, *Charles Bukowski's Underwood Champion*, Temporary wall sculpture. 2013.

One of the most singular aspects of Youd's project is the contrast between the extreme materiality and seriality of the process, on the one hand, and the supremely elusive nature of the result, on the other. The artist takes on the activity of the modern transcriber, the deskbound typist whose mind can be elsewhere as long as he or she keeps pounding the keys. Or the *Bouvard et Pécuchet*-like subjectivity of Santiago Badariotti. I've had the opportunity to observe Youd for a bit as he was retyping William Faulkner's *The Sound and the Fury*, and I noticed that his state of mind was far from the romantic ideal of creation or the programmatic ecstasy of a self-propelling conceptual project. The performance was accompanied by details that accentuated the pedestrian and even slightly profane character of the task: headphones for working, fruit and yogurt for his lunch break.

The extravagance of the project lay in his making the novel fit onto a single page. It's difficult to know how Youd deals with typing errors (which could range from a spelling mistake to a skipped line); but given that the final product is illegible, the number and scope of these errata is ultimately irrelevant. Even if one believes in the honesty of the performance and Youd's mechanical skill (which is to say, that the result is indeed a literal transcription of *The Sound and the Fury*), the culmination of the work in a flat blackened piece of paper means that the novel and the performance are at once on full display and hidden beyond all means of verification.

In other words, it's a copy whose method precludes the possibility of confirming its fidelity to the referent: the rectangular stain 'is' *The Sound and the Fury* chiefly because of the performative signature of the artist, since the performance itself entails the destruction of the copy as a legible form. In a certain sense, Youd materializes the chaos inherent in any textual chain, threatened by the eventual disaggregation of the sequence of letters that it conjoins (Borges' infantile fear when faced with the printed page). Additionally, from my perspective, this also suggests that Youd's motley pages are akin to books that have never been opened. In fact, they are similar to what we would get by projecting multiple scans of each page of a book on a single surface.

At the same time, the second part of Youd's diptych appears to be the trace or residue of the mechanical inscription. Is it a metaphor of reading, understood as the everchanging echo of the original? It could also be seen as a sign. Youd inhabits a different territory to Kacero. But both choose to centre their work on the almost private intersection between writing and literature.

My encounter with both projects was fortuitous. I found out about Kacero's work through a brilliant post by Matías Serra Bradford on the blog of the publisher Eterna Cadencia,[13] and, as I mentioned, I witnessed Youd in action at Rowan Oak, the William Faulkner house and museum in Oxford, Mississippi.[14] It was a fortuitous encounter because I had already been writing for years about the nature of writing at a time when digital modes were changing the concept and meaning of a physical original. These works allowed me to confirm the relevance of these issues, insofar as they also seemed to preoccupy artists coming from the visual arts; furthermore, perhaps a bit selfishly, I could consider them to be epiphenomena of my own concerns. The projects were so germane that I decided to incorporate them into these notes on a topic that is at once extremely vast and absolutely central to the aesthetic practice of contemporary writers.

---

13   Matías Serra Bradford, 'Apuntes prepóstumos para un artista que actúa de muerto', at blog.eternacadencia.com.ar/archives/37983.
14   More information on the performance can be point on the following University of Mississippi webpage: museum.olemiss.edu/ timyoud-retypes-the-sound-and-the-fury.

Seven. For years I transcribed my classes in the university. I would carry an old cassette recorder with me and sit near the professor. At night I would type out what I heard on the tape. The typewriter itself was relatively old, made from wrought iron with Bakelite keys that needed to be pressed deeply and with force. Rather than use regular paper, I wrote on stencil sheets designed for making copies on a mimeograph machine. I would remove the ink ribbon and let the type hammer simply punch into the hectograph paper.[15] Each class would produce sixteen to eighteen pages more properly described as cast than written – a bit in the style of Youd, though not quite as radical. I remember finding tiny paper remainders everywhere; a little smaller and they would have been dust. Since the type hammers often accumulated sediment from the repeated impact against the paper, each letter had to be cleaned regularly with alcohol and a pin in order to remove as much excess material as possible.

At the same time, it was important to avoid too many errors; otherwise I would waste both the stencil paper and all of the transcription work I had done upon it. To make corrections, I would apply white-out to the affected area, using the miniature brush affixed to the cap of the bottle. I would spread a thin layer of white-out, wait for it to dry, and then write the new text over it. A mistake of more than a few centimetres, for instance a skipped word or a poorly articulated phrase, could render corrections impossible, since the wider the white strip extended, the stickier the type hammers got, and the more indecipherable the new writing became.

---

15 This led to some curious effects, because sometimes, when I went back to using the typewriter normally, I would forget to reattach the ink ribbon and the paper would retain the ghostly impressions of the type hammers.

In addition to all of these precautions I also had to deal with the gradual thickening of the white-out. Since the white-out contained an alcoholic solution that allowed it to dry quickly, the remaining fluid became denser with every use. It would eventually start to build up on the stencil paper, like a half-finished plaster job or a small-scale detail of one of the monumental works of Rafael Bueno or Anselm Kiefer, with thick accretions of material on the surface. Occasionally the stencil papers would acquire numerous horizontal bands of decorative paste, whose whitish mass absorbed the light and often seemed to obscure the typed words rather than reveal them.

There is an adjective we use a lot in Argentina that describes the outcome of this process perfectly: *desprolijo*, messy. But the aim was to extract from this activity some sort of aesthetic quality, however illusory. The point at which the writing and the object merged together. To describe the process now may make it seem like this was merely preparatory work. But it continues to inform my writing, almost as a kind of origin point. One of those actions that we are not fully conscious of in the moment, but that project themselves into the future, even as they are later replaced by other practices. I detail this not simply out of professional pride – that is, to show that I acted like a scribe before I became a writer – but also to signal the reminiscent power one can feel when confronted by objects or installations connected to mechanical writing.

For instance, long before I started destroying stencil paper, Carl Andre composed a series of poems with typewriters using what critics have referred to as a sculptural style. When I saw some of these diagrammatic compositions recently, my first thought was naturally of concrete poetry; but upon learning that many of the sculptures had been done in the sixties, it wasn't hard for me to associate them with my own childhood, insofar as, when given the opportunity, I would play with a typewriter in a similar way to Andre. Both of us took maximum advantage of the tabulators and the fixed margins for characters. (These simple typewriter functions must be the only ones that became more complicated with contemporary word processors, which require special applications for these functions.) But Andre obviously took into account the words that he used as foundations for those constructions, and in so doing posited the presence of a material aspect to them, a materialism distinct from the one found in objects, but tangible nonetheless.[16]

Eight. Our relationship to writing is both practical and abstract. The observations I've just shared, and the memories associated with them – including the one I'll mention in a moment – have led me to believe that writers typically understand their relationship to literature and books exclusively in terms of intellectual coexistence, even when this is vaguely defined. Nevertheless, in many cases it seems crucial to focus on the more practical dimension of literary work as well, by which I mean the pragmatism inherent in the act of writing itself. Our relationship to writing emanates from rituals and procedures as well as intellectual operations, and many of these can be empirically described – a fact that obviously extends to digital writing and editing. One intriguing characteristic of digital formats is the link that they establish between text and simulation.

One day I was talking to a writer, also called P, who has never composed on anything but word processors. We were discussing what each of us was currently working

16   Cf. Claire Gilman, 'Drawing Time, Reading Time', in *Drawings Papers* 108, The Drawing Center, New York, 2014.

on. At some point the usual question arose about our respective writing practices. Typically, these conversations follow a short and predetermined script: schedule, more or less dysfunctional habits, fetishes, tics, etc. I said that at a certain point using a word processor had become natural for me, since it's what best emulates writing by hand, with regard to the freedom to rearrange parts of the text and also in terms of immediacy. Writing on the computer can be incredibly gratifying and absorbing.

The comment must have piqued P's curiosity, because he wanted to know how I wrote before I started using a computer. The question opened up a horizon of memories not exactly hidden but zealously partitioned: each reminiscence seemed to come from a vanished past, or better yet, a forgotten topography of the earth.

IBM Selectric typeball and daisy wheel
for an electric typewriter

The question also triggered gusts of conflicting memories and impressions, perhaps the most curious of which was my perception, while I was speaking, that my interlocutor was unaware of aspects of writing prior to the computer. It was almost as if he were encountering for the first time the extravagant customs of a bygone era.

In a few short years I had gone through various kinds of typewriters. I was constantly updating my writing equipment, in a seemingly endless process without a clear end in sight. I wrote on old typewriters that required unusual finger strength (as I mentioned earlier), on electric typewriters that prematurely aged and were inadequate precursors to the computer, on typewriters that used the 'daisy wheel' system. To speak only of mechanical typewriters, I progressed from classic machines to second-hand portable ones, but only after trying out the medium-sized desktop models, light brown Olivettis that could be found on nearly every desk in Argentina in the seventies and eighties.

I explained to my friend everything about the ink, the bi-coloured ribbons, the spools, the line space selector, the tabulators and the spaces, the sounds, etc. P listened without judgement. He hadn't expected such a detailed response. But I was possessed, not only by the rhetoric of nostalgia but also by the rhetoric of identity. I recalled the built-up sediment on the type hammers (as I mentioned before), whose tiny swirls and perforations accumulated so much material that they began to impart large blots on the page that looked like obese versions of the original letters. I added that for me the typewriter had been a tool fraught with all sorts of mechanical problems, serviceable only by means of an arsenal of auxiliary equipment. It was only when the computer arrived that I appreciated the simplicity and naturalness of writing by hand – having nonetheless given up the practice many years prior.[17]

---

17   I highly recommend Friedrich Kittler's study of the spread of the typewriter from the nineteenth century onward, which focuses on the industrial proliferation of the machine, on the one hand, and the new problems associated with writing, on the other. The typewriter, as an instrument or obstacle for writing and as a tool that authors used directly or indirectly (if they were dictating to someone

I then gave him an overview of the 'golf ball' typewriters of the IBM Selectric line, those veritable emblems of corporate industry whose nickname derives from the small metal sphere covered in characters that rotates each time before striking the page.[18] Finally, following these IBMs, the electronic typewriters arrived, flat and light by comparison.[19]

These operating protocols were vague and incomprehensible to my friend. His response to my account of my typewriting history was to oscillate between a kind of borrowed nostalgia and total disbelief. I often find myself conveying forms of knowledge that are either extinct or

---

else), had a decisive impact on the aesthetic and conceptual imagination linked to creation and character. For instance, the Nietzschean phrase that stands as the epigraph to this book, and which alludes to his use of a typewriter as well as to his adoption of an aphoristic style, is an argumentative leitmotif of Kittler's work. Friedrick A. Kittler, *Gramophone, Film, Typewriter*, Stanford: Stanford University Press, 1999.

18   The little ball moved back and forth along the stationary roller. It rotated into position and the type hammer struck with a dry sound on the ribbon that resembled the violent smack of a riveter. I pointed out – perhaps redundantly – that a large portion of the history of writing is the history of blows to a surface.

19   On the upper part of the keyboard there was a horizontal digital text display where one could read what one was writing. Properly speaking, the 'daisy wheel' was a small plastic disc, with a serrated hole in the middle, attached to a piece of metal that moved across the roller (which was also stationary). The daisy wheel rotated and, depending on which key was pressed, the corresponding 'petal' would strike the roller (on top of the ribbon). Along the perimeter of the daisy wheel there were multiple petals, that is, flexible rods at the end of which the characters were stamped (each character a lower-case or upper-case letter, a number or a symbol). Thus, one had the option of changing the typography, replacing one daisy wheel with another that had a different set of letters (the same option existed on several models of the IBM golf ball line).

in the process of disappearing – and isn't that what literature does as well? This was one of those moments, like when ex-smokers expound upon their former rituals of lighting up: the objects they used to assist them, the theatricality of smoking, their relationship to accessories, etc. In fact, not unlike cigarettes, typewriters demanded a whole set of manual operations.[20] Contemporary word processors, on the other hand, require only the use of our fingertips; they have become so exclusively tactile that they seem completely divorced from any idea of manipulation. Their capacity for abstraction lies in the sheer passivity with which we can employ them, similar to how our hand forms letters when writing things out, without our even thinking about it.[21]

Nine. As I've explained, writing today entails fewer practical challenges and implies a different relationship to our ideas and presuppositions about its nature. My memory of typewritten manuscripts is of different phases

---

20   Significantly, I gave up smoking at the same time that I began to adapt to the computer. It was as if the dematerialization of my writing naturally eradicated those habits that relied on mechanical or material aids.

21   Moreover, I recall the short transition period between the typewriter and the word processor, which we now almost singularly associate with Microsoft Word. These were the years when Word Perfect was the main word processing application for computers, which primarily ran on DOS, since Windows was far from being the dominant operating system at the time. The type of commands that one performed in Word Perfect through various combinations of letters and symbols, the absence or ineffectiveness of the mouse, and more than anything the screen that did not correspond in format or design to the written document (unlike in the case of Word) – all of this made the experience of writing on a computer a far more abstract activity, free from the mimetic ideal to which it would later become attached.

of manual composition that necessitated various 'office supplies', tools that all seem a bit amateurish now. My impression of electronic texts, on the other hand, is that, first and foremost, they come into being as reverberations of a source that cannot be attributed to any physically verifiable place.

I assume that this difference translates into a distinct relationship with the written word and a distinct approach to its practice. I'm alluding here to the extreme materiality of the earlier writing process – the physical work of proofing, the material production, the collation of various versions, etc. – in contrast to current digital operations, which are relatively undifferentiated insofar as they can almost all be achieved by means of a keyboard and do not require a change in format in order to move from one compositional stage to another.

The intangibility of the written word often returns us to the unstable – and similarly intangible – relationship that writing establishes with what it intends to say. Immaterial writing, i.e. that which we see on the screen when we work on texts (all sorts of texts, not just literary ones), possesses a state of latency and even reflexivity that was lacking in a previous era, when texts appeared in physical form and their material manifestation was the only guarantee of their preservation. To a certain extent they were 'true'; they formed a tangible part of the contingent world, in the sense that they were supported by a specific physical operation that had given them life.

On the other hand, I find that the more transitory and vaguely incandescent nature of digital writing relies on an even more abstract and mysterious dimension, as if the only characteristics it could borrow from physical writing were negative ones. Each kind of writing has a different disposition. Physical writing is alert, always adjusting to what happens around it, unable to evade a whole series of consecutive steps. Digital writing, on the other hand, maintains a stony indifference to the accidental nature of composition and what it has left behind, that is, whatever is on our side of the screen. Henceforth I will refer to the different dispositions of textual forms as their 'pensive presence'. Jacques Rancière speaks of the 'pensive image' when referring to certain photos whose meaning is detached from the intentionality of the photographer. The 'pensiveness' of an image consists of a dimension that is autonomous from both the creator and the viewer, a sort of excess or residue, depending on whose viewpoint we take, and that can be understood as a reflexive and permanently unstable condition. Rancière says:

> A pensive image is an image that contains unthought thought, a thought that cannot be attributed to the intention of the person who produces it and that has an effect on the person who views it without that person linking it to a determinate object. Pensiveness thus refers to a condition that is indeterminately between the active and the passive.[22]

Here I adopt the idea of the 'pensive presence' of writing as a metaphor for the effect of immaterial textuality. As I mentioned earlier, physical, material writing is directly opposed to immaterial, digital writing in terms of its inscription and its afterlife. The pensiveness of digital writing would derive from the fact that, though immaterial itself, it endlessly simulates the conditions of material writing. In this sense, digital writing is indeed

22   Jacques Rancière, *The Emancipated Spectator*, trans. Gregory Elliott, New York: Verso, 2008.

defined by an analogue; not to its discursive referents, however, but to the textual forms that preceded it.

I like the idea of conferring a bit of dynamism upon a seemingly given object, passive in the sense of being fixed and unmodifiable, although potentially eloquent, like the photographic image. I would say that digital writing behaves like a nucleus of activity at an embryonic stage, though passively, as if throwing off indecipherable glances.

I suppose that Rancière designates this condition as 'pensive' because the unstable meaning of the photographs themselves, which in the cases he analyses exhibit specific physical and temporal traits, conscripts them into an ambiguous order. They are omnipresent and elusive at the same time. Additionally, perhaps because of this silent dynamism of the pensive image, which I associate with a tremor (albeit an unlocalizable one), it also emanates a sense of doubt, almost a psychological disposition, on the part of certain photographs. In some sense, doubt is the most self-reflexive and emotional gesture of thought. Thus immaterial writing might be considered to overcome the fragility of its virtual condition through this self-reflexive, doubtful disposition.

Ten. Some years ago I started writing a blog. I posted things intermittently, or carelessly, or perhaps a bit of both; I think I still use the blog in the same way. In any case, its existence, tangential for the most part to my primary projects, has changed the way I understand my own writing. The blog is composed of different kinds of writing. I don't maintain it as a place to voice my opinions or make announcements about my books. I take advantage of the free space and set templates in order to post textual fragments, essays, and other forms of writing. The comments section isn't activated and there aren't links to any other webpages. It's something of an autistic site, one that seeks to be as stealthy as possible.

At first I saw the blog primarily as a forum for people to read my writing. But later I began to realize that this reservoir of online texts, silent though it was, inspired me to write, simply because of the persistence of its presence.[23]

Thus on the one hand we have the printed word, published mostly in book format, which is to say, at least in the majority of cases, on paper; on the other hand, we have the virtual word, available to anyone with a digital screen. The printed word necessarily exists in a fossilized state; books make up the cemetery we call the library, easy to access but already symbolically muted by the very nature of their material form. The common ailments that all books suffer, for instance the yellowing of the paper, speak to the strange expiration date that marks them as objects. Nevertheless, they retain a certain stability: the clearer the risk of their disintegration, the more monumental their material presence seems to be.

On the blog I become my own editor, a slightly different role from the one I play when I'm working with my own manuscripts. The webpage allows me to avoid the format of the book and other related entities, as well as to combine texts from a whole range of

---

23   In this sense, the metaphorical use of 'hosting' to refer to the provision of space and memory on a server seems entirely appropriate to me. There is something wicked and parasitic about enjoying the hospitality of a host. It suggests a kind of inertia, or clandestine existence – an attitude somewhere between stealthy and sneaky. To be hosted is to be in a provisional state – otherwise we would describe it in some other way – and therefore to be suspicious. A strange feeling to have your text 'hosted' on a site, as if its presence were temporary, though in fact it can continue indefinitely.

different registers. Nothing prevents me, for instance, from giving textual fragments of a novel the exact same title as photographs of those textual fragments. The image of my handwritten 'original' gives off more of an aura than a typed version of the text, but the digital format grants it a more enigmatic – and I'd say genuine or self-sufficient – character that seems to protect it from all worldly harm.

As inert objects waiting for the code that will revive them, virtual texts find refuge in a wilderness that nevertheless guarantees their immutability – unlike printed texts, which are chained to time and the physical degradations of the world. That's why each kind of text has such a different disposition. Digital texts (by which I mean texts on a flat screen, without any significant design features; a stream of letters roughly and inescapably formatted to the width of that very same screen) hold out the promise of permanence without change. At times latent and at other times simply lethargic, electronic writing affords an access that appears to be constant but is always equivocal. On the other hand, printed writing tends to rest on a different kind of plane: that of hierarchies and certainties, that of graphic design, archives, catalogues and classifications, in other words, the material organization of things.

In a certain sense, I think that my writing gets along better with the features of digital presence than physical presence. That's why I'm sometimes tempted to post texts online, because there they can enjoy a continuous existence and, at least to all appearances, remain oblivious to worldly travails. The joy of forgetting and persisting at the same time.

Detour: Examples

I would like to propose an example of how the nature of the written (and our attitudes toward writing) changes when a text shifts from a printed version to a digital format. I will refer to an empirical test I recently undertook with some lines from Antonio Di Benedetto's *Zama*, a novel for which I possess the most profound affection and admiration, feelings that naturally extend toward the author himself.

The following is a close-up of the page that contains one of the excerpts, below which is the same text transcribed in 'Notes' – that is, a word processing program with almost no text formatting options – reproduced in the form of a screen capture.

> Recién comenzaba la tarde y tanto mal me había dado aquel día que me espantaba continuarlo. Pero no se puede renunciar a vivir medio día: o el resto de la eternidad o nada.

> Recién comenzaba la tarde y tanto mal me había dado aquel día que me espantaba continuarlo. Pero no se puede renunciar a vivir medio día: o el resto de la eternidad o nada.

A comparison of the two yields interesting results. It would be bold to claim that they don't say the same thing. And yet, their different material states contribute to semantic echoes that are not fully analogous. This is due to the fact that the same textual sequence can produce a distinct visual feel that inclines us toward a different reading of accent and intonation.

My impression is that each format enacts a different relationship toward the real, both in what they say and what they allow themselves to say. The divergence does not arise from their relations to an objective truth or to the truth of the events articulated by the novel, but rather to the distinct ways in which each graphic iteration points toward an affective context. As is well known, the same phrase doesn't always mean the same thing – to the contrary. Here again is the quotation (this time in Esther Allen's English translation):

> The afternoon was barely underway and yet the day had already brought such troubles that I was terrified to go on. But a man cannot renounce his life for half a day. There is either the rest of eternity or nothing.[24]

The last part in particular is a formulation typical of Saint Augustine's *Confessions*. Nevertheless, beyond any similarities one might posit between the two formats, I find that the 'printed' version establishes a link to the definite and postulates a more conclusive meaning than the one produced by the screen capture, a chain of letters with such a lack of density and immateriality that it suggests a more hypothetical statement.

These divergent emphases result from the pensive presence associated with digital writing. The difference in the visual appearance and support also renders distinct verbal intonations in each format, as if there were distinct affective registers in the very same text. The printed presence is more sombre and unbending; the electronic one is more unstable and secretive, of a lightweight consistency that seems to be on guard because it's hiding something. Is this because the screen capture retains the feel of something recently written and therefore subject to change? Of something that runs the risk of returning to an earlier formulation or even disappearing entirely,

---

24 Antonio Di Benedetto, *Zama*, trans. Esther Allen. New York: New York Review Books, 2016.

depending on the temperament of the finger that converted it into digital form?

The reproduction of the text published on paper, meanwhile, takes on all of the characteristics of permanence and intangibility that the unstable version, the digital version, is unable to guarantee. This is true to such an extent that it is difficult to think of these two modes as anything but Machiavellian inversions of one another. In the case of the printed text, its material presence indicates a strong relationship to the notion and practice of archiving central to the historical accumulation of knowledge and information. This is obviously a marker of the longstanding complicity between classification systems and the printed word. On the other hand, the non-printed text reveals the destabilization inherent in all immaterial writing, which is generically shifty compared to conventional archival material.

Perhaps this simple visual comparison between the two formats illustrates the battle between those modes that stabilize writing in order to guarantee existing forms of knowledge (and above all the relationships among them), and those that point to the disarticulation of the hierarchies of the letter as the sign of a new narrative and scientific genre.

There has always been friction between the variable domain of the written word and the 'fixed' world of reality. Philosophy, literature, and their related fields all reflect this. But digital writing destabilizes even this opposition. The fluid and unstable nature of the digital sphere has begun to infiltrate the preserve of the archive and the notion of the fossilized collection that surrounds material writing, destructuring the world of the printed book consecrated by the copy and the reproduction.

Eleven. The printed word is opposed to the pensive presence of writing. The hegemony of print, associated historically with the systemization of knowledge and discourses, including those that challenged the dominant ones, has made the silencing of the pensive presence of handwritten and digital writing one of the conditions of its existence. It is the guarantor of its dominant position as a writing format, of its proverbial adaptability to the categories used in the administration and classification of archival documents. The power exerted by the written word is so ironclad that even the most 'pensive' textual forms end up being disciplined by it.

Perhaps one of the only options for creating a kind of writing that preserves that initial surge of pensiveness would be to channel these alternative graphic energies (whether manual or digital) into different narrative operations and forms. This would allow for a new mode of literary composition at its most constructive, one that reflected the hesitancy and instability inherent to all writing.

In this respect, *pensiveness* would refer to a secondary capacity for narration or reflexivity within the telling of the story itself. By virtue of its own hypothetical register and expansive scope, that capacity might rescue the story from the danger of remaining enclosed within the universe of literature and the ossification of meaning.

If this is indeed the case, we could identify a more or less silent conflict between these two conceptions of writing. In general terms, between an assertive writing (fixed by the institutions linked to print and the book) and a non–assertive writing (more fluid and less defined, sometimes conceptual, deriving its unstable condition from the skill of the hand or the capacities of the machine).[25]

25   Of course, we cannot overlook the corporations and institutions that stand behind internet sites and the internet itself, working in

This obviously represents an unequal struggle, in which the unstable models can only be successful if they transform themselves into narrative formats and conceptual styles that, in terms of meaning and the prosodic cadence associated with syntax, attempt to break through the fossilization of the printed word even when they must resort to it in order to impose a different textual regime or condition.

Twelve. Some digital formats challenge the principle of sequentiality. If we understand the digital to encompass that which is interactive and textually unstable, that which does not acquire a physical presence and therefore could conceivably be destroyed at any moment, those forms of collective creation generated in the so-called digital humanities will affect our view of literature more generally.

One of the most immediate effects of the digital humanities, aside from the erasure of the borders among certain frameworks, disciplines and modes of circulation and textual formatting, is the simultaneous destabilization of the idea of the author as a determining category of the work, and of the idea of the finished work itself. The work now seems to consist of a cumulative series of operations, textual strategies, and classificatory decisions, all of which are constantly in flux and organized at various levels of composition, and many of which raise questions about authorship.

I wonder if something analogous would be possible

_____

various capacities, dematerialized but also tangible in terms of processes and protocols, creating the illusion of a virtual world in which all values and interests are flexible. The scope of my investigation here, however, is limited to the screen as a formatting device for writing. For the most part, and at its most effective, this word processing activity takes place offline.

in literature: are there multiple forms of writing that would annul our typical idea of the author? I think the answer is both yes and no. On the one hand, I believe that a good number of 'digital humanities' projects could be likened to literature, in the sense that they 'design' their own readers and incorporate conceptual challenges that could very well be applied to the frameworks of fiction and aesthetic discursivity. On the other hand, I'm not sure whether these formats can inaugurate a precise subjectivity that would allow for the creation of an idea of the reader that would more or less converge with that modality.

From a different point of view, I suppose that immaterial writing – that is, writing in a virtual format – finds its fullest realization as an event through electronic circulation, which is also virtual, because, like all literature, its material presence paradoxically coexists with its immaterial one, by virtue of the fact that a text may be conserved even if its original is destroyed.

In addition, the digital dimension situates on the same plane different kinds of texts that in the realm of physical publication tend to remain separate, because they require the schema of the book, the institutional imprimatur represented by editing and cataloguing, in order to make themselves legible as operative texts. I'm referring here to notes, diaries, letters, private writings, and incomplete compositions more generally. These kinds of writing can now circulate instantaneously. And yet in many cases their compositional form and mode of conservation imply that they don't exist as such, insofar as these marginal texts, written without a material support, often become definitively ephemeral, or entirely irrelevant, since their relevance is derived precisely from their physical precarity or volatility. Perhaps I will return to this later. For now, it is enough to examine the strictly digital effects of digital texts, how they influence not only the phase of writing but also the phases of conception and construction.

Thirteen. Sometimes narration uses imitation as a means of defining itself against the backdrop of the general disintegration of discursive boundaries. Given our increasing immersion in electronic modalities of reading and writing, a certain alchemy can be achieved by mixing digital paradigms with more traditional forms of narrative representations. I'm thinking here of a series of three texts by Agustín Fernández Mallo titled 'Mutaciones'.[26] Each text reconstructs a journey taken and previously described by someone else. One such journey is that recounted by Robert Smithson in his well-known essay 'A Tour of the Monuments of Passaic'. The title of Fernández Mallo's text is 'A Tour of *The Monuments of Passaic* 2009'.

Smith's essay describes his visit to a spot on the Passaic River, in New Jersey, through a series of reflections on the landscape and photographs taken *in situ*. Fernández Mallo's text reconstructs Smithson's tour, but it also explores the essay itself through comparisons, citations, and references. In the style of many other contemporary journalists, documentarians, and researchers, who track the prior itineraries of naturalists, explorers, and navigators, Fernández Mallo retraces the steps of a notable precursor. But Fernández Mallo's reconstruction, though mimetic, is not literal. He uses Google Maps and Google Earth.

From the beginning of the text, one recognizes that the whole sequence of narrative topoi relating to the description of a voyage (preparations, changes in itinerary,

---

26   A. Fernández Mallo, *El Hacedor, de Borges (Remake)*, Madrid: Alfaguara, 2001, pp. 58–99.

meetings, wrong turns, discoveries, etc.) is deployed by Fernández Mallo through virtual coordinates and visual reproductions. His narrator journeys through and alongside the screen, and the 'small hand with the white glove' that functions as a cursor strikes him both as a sign of the times and a symbol of his own subjectivity as a traveller.[27] At the same time, the images reproduced in the text oscillate between Smithson's original photographs and those taken by the author with his cell phone during his 'journey' in front of the computer screen.

Among the many questions raised by the text, I'm particularly interested in the one concerning literature as a system predisposed to adopt the principles and protocols of simulation. Simulation consists of an imitative structure whereby each element taken from reality performs a necessarily analogical function. We could say that it is a 'representation' only if we restrict the meaning of that word. Simulation, on the other hand, demands a direct and unbroken link with the world that is being imitated. A simulation can certainly recreate closed or non-existent systems, but it must always obey the rules that govern them as if it were subjecting itself to the rules of reality.

The use of simulators has ranged from military training to pedagogical exercises, and includes the whole field of video and computer games that are devoted, at least in principle, to entertainment and play. Nevertheless, all these different kinds of simulators imply a specific narrative syntax. Fernández Mallo's 'Mutaciones' fit

27 'I return to Google Maps, and zoom in on the map of the area. The Google Maps icon, which glides across the screen as you move the mouse, is not an arrow but a hand with a white glove [inevitably, my first memory during this stroll is of Michael Jackson, who died just a few days ago]. Now I'm going over the first monument-bridge (...)' A. Fernández Mallo, 61.

the definition of simulations, I believe, insofar as their digital efforts (observation through the computer, physical exploration through the digital map, documentation through the cell phone camera) seek a narrative framework that depicts the real world through analogy and iconicity rather than through representation.

Fernández Mallo's narrator reconstructs Smithson's original journey through the use of images from two different moments and the conceptual observations of the 'original' author. But it should also be said that, given the indirect way that the original material is verified, a new conceptualization emerges from this digital approach. The result is a cartography that is at times ironic and at times exact, but that never entirely functions as a true re-enactment.

I have the sense that texts like Fernández Mallo's reveal a burgeoning literary mode, one that also intervenes in the canons of literature as a whole (insofar as it proceeds by rereading works of the past, not simply by creating new works or compositional strategies in the present). Literature no longer – or no longer only – functions as a representational strategy but as a mode of simulation, not unlike a digital map or even a videogame. Simulation allows for the possibility of operating upon existing represented worlds – including those worlds represented on screen that find their governing logic in a set of analogical and iconic references to reality.

When translated into the realm of literature, this system could be described as another kind of realism, which encounters in the practice of simulation a framework for new sensibilities and subjectivities, derived from distinct kinds of testimonies, beliefs, and vicarious experiences.

Reality Effects

Usually literature, or more properly, narrative literature, is not an art of actual images. This fact allows for narrative complexity when it comes to descriptions in general and ekphrasis more specifically. Narrative seeks to offer visual imagery while knowing that a truly mimetic outcome is close to impossible. Nevertheless, the one aspect of the literary that does possess a close relationship to the visual in terms of iconicity is the handwritten manuscript. Original manuscripts have obviously been objects of interest for philologists and genetic critics, who study them for clues about the systemization of writing and its dissemination. But in their capacity as 'originals', they have also come to represent the auratic and irreplaceable source of the work – despite the fact that the work, given its discursive condition, does not inherently contain the idea of a material original. The physical manuscript, therefore, has always been perceived as a guarantor of truth, both in its analogous capacity as a substrate and as a material object in the world.

Fourteen. The virtuality of digital writing makes it an ambiguous threat. As I mentioned above, immaterial writing (represented paradigmatically by the computer screen) encodes a friction between immutability (the promise of perpetual presence and the absence of material deterioration) and fragility (the risk of a sudden collapse that would destroy the archive, and the constant danger of variation). There is an afterlife suggested by immaterial writing that is different from the afterlife suggested by material writing. Material writing persists as an inscription on reality, on actual objects, and therefore it exhibits or prefigures its eventual death. Immaterial writing, on the other hand, tends to evade libraries and catalogues – not always successfully, but always in conflict with the notion of the material original. These distinct and arguably novel conditions of writing also have consequences for our ideas about literary realism.

I'm interested in this double consistency of handwritten manuscripts because, in the years since the ascendancy of word processors, the inventory of manuscripts has irrevocably diminished. I don't just mean manuscripts of literary works, but also the entire paratextual apparatus: annotations, letters, diaries, etc. That whole grab bag of textual forms that in the case of canonized writers take on a sort of talismanic power that complements and occasionally substitutes for the work itself. What is revealed with the virtual disappearance of the manuscript is not so much the lack of a physical format for lineated text, since most authors and critics themselves have turned their backs on the supposed truth of the handwritten text, but rather the loss of the aura surrounding the original.

One sign of the disintegration of this auratic presence is the very veneration with which handwriting itself is increasingly treated. More and more frequently we see exhibitions organized around written manuscripts; they are now collected with greater zeal and bought with more money. A larger number of artistic installations involve calligraphic elements – the aforementioned project of Fabio Kacero, for example, and others I will discuss shortly. Even the documentary value of manuscripts has changed: since they can now be copied, scanned and magnified in their minutest details, we see them almost as a kind of artistic venture – as if they were unexpected and at times miraculous additions to the work, rather than artefacts of merely philological interest.[28]

28 In 2013, there was a commemoration of the hundredth anniversary of the publication of *Swann's Way*, the first volume of *In*

Thus, similar to what Roland Barthes said about certain photographs, the original would simply be that which occurred at the right time and place. Taking this logic to its extreme, we could affirm that the presence of the original announces more than anything else that the author did not write everything that he or she could have written, and that the script that we possess is not undeniable proof of intellectual rumination (nor of course of a critical consciousness) but rather of the effect of daily, pedestrian

---

Search of Lost Time. The exhibit included notebooks with the original manuscripts, galley proofs corrected by the author, drafts, letters, related writings, and also some postcards from the period that had served as inspiration for Proust. As often happens with phenomena that attract so much popular attention, the spectator's gaze is drawn more to the crowd than to the object itself. That's what happened to me both times I tried to see the exhibition. In one sense, I could say that I wasn't able to see it at all due to the sheer number of people massed around the display cases and framed objects. In another sense, though, I felt as if, in observing the faces of the public, I was actually getting a *better view* of the materials and the true meaning they possessed. The visitors gave off something like anxiety – respect of course, but it was mixed with a curious enjoyment, at first glance vacant, neither religious nor aesthetic, perhaps moral, though at the same time distracted, interrupted, or fatigued. They were looking for an instant truth, some kind of a revelation produced by their physical proximity to the written words and those objects upon which Proust had placed his sacred touch. This reverential atmosphere was so intense and almost funeral-like – though also easily disturbed at moments – and the care with which the papers and drawings were being preserved was so zealous, that the people coming and going seemed too tired to engage in any abstract speculations, which ended up making the event itself seem highly abstract. The exhibit obeyed the logic of the museum, but the materials appealed to the practices of the library. There was thus an implicit competition between looking and reading, which, given the museumification of the exhibit's contents – and Proust's diminutive handwriting – was clearly won by those who were looking. 'Marcel Proust and Swann's Way: 100th Anniversary,' Morgan Library and Museum, February 15-April 28, 2013, New York.

ritual. We could also affirm that the gap between the unconscious pull of the hand as one writes and the transcendent value ascribed to those handwritten works deemed worthy of conservation is precisely what fascinates us when we contemplate the manuscripts of famous writers, because it is through this contemplation that we realize that all writing is originally accidental and prosaic. The aura of the literary does not simply emerge from the physical act of transcription; it is something else that elevates it and rescues it from indeterminacy – the mystery of beauty, the opinion of those in the know, literary history, the prestige of institutions, or simply the immediacy of the letters traced by a genius. This is why it is worth contemplating.

Fifteen. Boris Groys speaks of the dialectic surrounding the concept of the aura once technologies of reproduction allow for copies that closely resemble the original. Groys says:

> In fact, the aura, as described by Benjamin, only comes into being thanks to the modern technique of reproduction. That is, it emerges precisely at the moment it is fading. It is born precisely for the same reason that it disappears... The erasure of all visually recognizable differences between original and copy is always only a potential one because it does not eliminate another difference existing between them which, albeit invisible, is none the less decisive: the original has an aura that the copy lacks. The original has an aura because it has a fixed context, a well-defined place in space; through that particular place it is inscribed also in history as a singular, original object.[29]

29   Boris Groys, 2008. 'The Topology of Contemporary Art', in *Antinomies of Art and Culture: Modernity, Postmodernity, Contemporaneity*,

According to Groys, modern art is indissolubly wedded to the idea of creativity; hence the importance of the original as proof and support (modern art, that is, as opposed to the critical and deconstructive moment of postmodernism – both distinct from our contemporary moment, open and absent in the space beyond itself).

In the case of modern literature, given its complicated relationship to materiality, attitudes toward individual creativity have usually entailed some scepticism about the idea of the unique original. Some notable examples of this are Mallarmé's typographical notion that 'A throw of the dice will never abolish chance' and the fact that Joyce lengthened the text of *Ulysses* by forty percent while correcting the galleys. In both cases, albeit through different operations, we can see the effects of the technologies of serial reproducibility. In literature, we might say, inspiration comes in a reproduceable format. It's true that inspiration here is not a precise synonym for aura, nevertheless this kind of 'inverse appropriation' leaves an intriguing mark on the final product and even more so on its *source*.

We also witness the classic symbolic pressure of the textual original in Henry James' *The Aspern Papers*, where the dead author's papers imbue the one who possesses them with their imagined attributes, provided the owner recognizes their significance. Mallarmé, Joyce, and James offer three basic possibilities for negotiating the auratic in literature. Modern literary aura has an embedded aporia, due to the fact that as an art it has *always* needed to reproduce the original.

There are various ways to reposition the aura in literature (by this I'm referring to the resurrection of the manuscript by other means, the restoration of the halo

eds. Okwui Enwezor, Nancy Condee, Terry Smith, Durham: Duke University Press, 2008.

in the symbolic or imaginary realm). Even oft-critiqued naturalist or conversationalist conventions, which tend to suppress textual mediation, can be seen as working toward this end, insofar as they invoke ideas of authenticity and spontaneity that reanimate earlier forms of auratic transmission. Here I would like to mention one specific example of an appeal to the resurrection of the manuscript, one that figures discursively as a central element of a novel's plot.

The novel is Juan José Saer's *El entenado*. In it, the narrator unpacks the experience of the past with support from an extended environmental leitmotif: in numerous scenes, he juxtaposes a bowl of olives and a glass of wine (from which he partakes as he writes) with the contact of his pen on paper. He speaks of the rough surface, but also the sound of the pen as it advances across the page. The repetition of this topos not only naturalizes the presence of the narrator within the novel, including his self-reflexive flourishes; it also theatricalizes the conception of the original by directly underscoring its material condition.

Saer's decision is more closely related to the practices of the modernist writers mentioned above than to contemporary modes of writing. For me, one of the central questions that derives from the current techniques of writing that lack the material support of paper is about how they connect to the reinscription of the auratic through other means; which is to say, through the prosthetic substitution of a non-existent manuscript. My sense is that the absence of the original reverberates in the electricity of the screen, and that the somewhat funereal presence of digital writing, that untouchable script that might nonetheless collapse at any moment, creates a kind of slippery foundation in which the very instability of the format becomes the effective support of its flickering existence. This is the pensiveness of this kind of writing I mentioned above.

Sixteen. Sometimes this analogical foundation colonizes even the most realist of forms, for example, in texts whose construction and organization are dominated by a particular kind of verisimilitude that derives from the communicative structures of digital media. These narratives adopt the protocols of messaging apps, Twitter, and email, and incorporate subject lines, timestamps, and message fields – all for the purpose of 'representing' contemporary human interaction by way of a revitalized communicative sensibility. Such texts seem to point in two directions at the same time: to the epistolary form that has had such a decisive effect on literary history and to the visual iconography of the contemporary computer screen. Or to put it slightly differently, they appropriate digital tools in order to elaborate upon conventional literary modes.

In these kinds of visual reproductions, which draw from different fields and often correspond to an individual operation of the keyboard or new configuration of an image, the literary device perfectly replicates its digital equivalent. These are heavily mimetic strategies and perhaps a bit limited from a compositional perspective, in that they demonstrate a certain acritical passivity in relation to technological advances, from which they derive what we might call their graphic eloquence. In this sense, they are undoubtedly naturalistic. But in spite of all this, they still serve as a crucial signal: of the pressure exerted by these new formats, which might very well indicate the development of new kinds of verisimilitude.

In his classic essay on the reality effect, Barthes registers the presence in modern literature of certain details that are irrelevant to the development of plot.

These are typically descriptions of setting, ornamental flourishes, or aspects tangential to the main conflict. He does not stop at documenting this presence, however, but rather inscribes it within a broader aesthetic regime: these background details become the defining feature of successful realist discourse. This attitude toward verisimilitude has not always predominated, he maintains; for instance, there have been periods defined by pictorial regimes in which authors eschewed realist or psychological imperatives in their texts, relying instead on the dominant modes for conveying plausibility during that particular era.

I submit that the pensiveness of digital writing, that is, its particular condition of proliferation and consecration, has led to the appearance of texts that belong to a new discursive regime of verisimilitude, one that constructs underground connections to traditional realism, but that nevertheless pursues a novel kind of realist configuration grounded in the digital arts.

I would like to refer to two projects, different among themselves, that nevertheless share a common conception of the textual plane, or simply the plane of the page or the screen, as a surface in which different elements of the real and the symbolic are negotiated. These projects are less concerned with narrative causality and development than they are with extracting materials from digital media that can serve as the basis for their textual construction and conceptual arc.

The texts that these projects yield tend to differ from those that we generally associate with the conventions of fiction or memoir, because they aspire to a realism detached from any sort of narrative impulse.

The first is an excerpt from one of the last books published by Lorenzo García Vega, *Son gotas del autismo visual,* which is dedicated to the testimony of his discontinuous experience as a 'visual narrator'.

Character 36 opens his eyes, and then finds himself in a desolate world.

Then I was faced with the green I once saw, in Chichén Itzá. The green, and a fog.
But from there other odours arise, other flavours, experienced earlier, many years earlier, in another place, in Central Australia, the mill of my childhood.

Chichén Itzá juxtaposed with Central Australia.
This hallucination affords me an extravagant visual tale.
- A postage stamp with a tiny wheat field alongside an orange sun, similarly tiny.

With the mouse cursor the tiny landscape on the postal stamp enlarges.
A click illuminates wheat and orange sun.

- To arrest, describe that strange moment in which, on a winter day, a piece of a luminous summer day inserts itself.
But what's backwards about the scene is the strange juxtaposition by which, during this strange moment, Gothic subtexts appear, brightening a vision of a building out of a horror movie where it's as if a character were being drawn in the same poem in which he tells his story.[30]

García Vega is essentially a performative author. He constructs his texts as if memories, intuitions and inclinations were all acoustic entities to be juxtaposed on the page, alongside historical and perceptual data. The idea is to arrange something like a verbal installation, one

30   Lorenzo García Vega, *Son gotas del autismo visual*, Guatemala City: Mata Mata Editions, 2010, pp. 75-76.

whose coherent manifestation in the real world would be impossible, as if each one of these elements assumed its own physical presence. This is why he was so inspired by the famous box art of Joseph Cornell, which he frequently mentions in his work.

In his work, he often creates time capsules (clear memories, and also hazy impressions or images from the past) and describes them as if they were concrete objects that possess an astonishing intelligibility – even for him – but often without ultimately including them in the scenes that he composes. His textual development may involve smells, temperature changes, sounds, the messages written on a store display window, images of sun-drenched trees or the cover of a book that he just read. Each one of these 'objects' is inscribed in a particular order, which may be modal, spatial, thematic, or otherwise. The unity of his work is the descriptive scene, the flexible and arboreal sequence that the text creates by subjecting different temporalities and registers to simultaneous cohabitation.

Thus, we could say that García Vega transposes Cornell's process to the computer screen. But to define his work in this way is to describe only half of the mystery, because he only takes from the screen the essential plot elements that he will use to construct a text free from normal temporal progression. There is a renunciation of narration, which is replaced by the simultaneous presentation of diverse materials. A 'plastic' narration, as García Vega himself used to say, elevated almost to the level of a proclamation in favour of a different concept of experience.

It's also worth mentioning in this context the works of Carlos Gradin (1980), several of which were collected in a volume that includes both poetry and prose.[31]

---

31   charly.gr, *(spam)*, Buenos Aires: Ediciones Stanton, 2011.

Gradin's primary compositional technique for nearly all of these works is the careful arrangement of 'results' from the Google search engine. Yet when we analyse Gradin's principles of selection for his system, it becomes clear that he is not merely seeking to develop an updated version of automatic writing.

In the first place, there's the figure of the author as digital address, 'charly.gr'. To my mind, this cannot simply be described as a pseudonym or likened to other standard devices for disguising or highlighting an author's identity, since the formulation explicitly establishes its resemblance to the proper name 'Carlos Gradin'. Rather, it seems like a gesture designed to explode the notion of the author itself, as if the subject who gives form to these materials refused to situate himself in the typical place of enunciation, choosing instead to see himself as a sort of robotic purveyor of content and textual links. I say 'sort of' because of the element of purpose in the composition, which, as in the case of many other conceptual projects, effectively separates questions about the construction of the piece from questions about the meaning of the contents we find therein.

Second, although the author called charly.gr alludes to his vocation as automaton and announces his algorithmic tendencies, he defines the search terms according to recognizable parameters, though the results themselves – which revolve around politics, colloquial speech, the world of fashion and entertainment, and certain historical icons – are not determined in advance. The most precise description of this compositional process might be that the author arranges textual installations using the search results derived from specific web queries. The subjective authorial element emerges in the selection of the search terms, over which Gradin throws a kind of magician's cloth. We cannot simply say that we're faced with a realist or confessional project, precisely because what this process highlights is the texture of the mediations (at once fortuitous and automatic) that arise between the choice of the terms and the result of the search.[32]

The back cover of *(spam)* is quite explicit about the modality of Gradin's text and its compositional strategies:

> The poems and texts that compose *(spam)* were generated through Google searches. The results were compiled and edited in the form of poetry or taken as starting points for prose texts. 'evening falls and', 'and I see the', 'Mau', 'these were the times of', 'Egyptian cigarettes', 'they will be days', 'I'm searching', 'greetings to' were the phrases that were entered into the search engine (in 'oldie games' no particular phrase was entered and not all phrases came from the search engine). The texts and searches were generated between May 2007 and July 2011.

Another frequently cited digital work by Gradin, avowedly installational and not conducive to the book format, is *El peronismo es como* ['Peronism is like']. Using the same procedures elaborated above, it organizes a prolonged sequence of phrases that the search engine has produced as results to a query. Against a plain green

---

32 Speaking of combinatorics, *Las lagunas inestables*, Milton Läufer's 'unpublished' novel, leaves the organization of certain passages up to the algorithmic whims of chance. These passages concern moments when the protagonist attempts to reconstruct his elusive past through a string of half-recalled memories. The grammatical structure of these fragments opposes the fixed format of the book, in that each successive download of the novel, which is hosted on the author's webpage, differs from the previous one. Naturally, this mechanism has consequences for the notion of the original text – digital or otherwise – which in this instance can be described as a unique and specific concatenation of words and phrases (www.miltonlaufer.com.ar/lagunas).

background, the text is generated while techno music plays. The results do not fill up the entire screen but rather appear successively on the same line (or occasionally two to three lines when the result is longer), spelled out letter by letter. Each result is the latter part of the expression 'Peronism is like', though the expression itself only appears at the very beginning.

There is, however, an element beyond its compositional method that identifies *El peronismo es como* with the new realist canon oriented toward digital verisimilitude. It involves the regularity of the work's metaphorical machinery, in which each entry appears quickly and just as quickly disappears. We are no longer dealing with the chaotic proliferation of likenesses spawned by the specific memory of a reader (who sees Peronism as 'like' various things), but rather of a textual enumeration that, though possibly chaotic in its conception, simulates in its presentation the clear yet transient syntax of the audio-visual form.[33]

Has realism become the most ephemeral of all literary simulations? García Vega and Gradin borrow from installation art to create their ephemeral works, and these works are thus difficult to replicate. García Vega's virtual boxes are impossible to reconstruct, as are the results from Gradin's online searches. This is a kind of literature that establishes a conflicted attitude toward temporality: given that it is based on writing, it should naturally tend toward permanence, but in fact it does the opposite.

33 Lately I've tried to visit the *El peronismo es como* page without success (Gradin has probably taken down the installation). To broaden the discussion about his project, I recommend a book by Juan José Mendoza on the digital avant-garde and an interesting article by Santiago Llach on poetry and politics: J.J. Mendoza, *Escrituras past. Tradiciones y futurismos del siglo 21*, Bahía Blanca: 17 grises, 2011; S. Llach, 'Lo que viene después', in *Pampa* n. 6, Buenos Aires, Sept 2010.

Another paragraph from the Groys essay refers to installations as the exemplary form of contemporary art:

> In a certain sense the installation is for our time what the novel was for the nineteenth century. The novel was a literary form that included all other literary forms of that time; the installation is an art form that includes all other contemporary art forms.

Groys speaks of the use of dissimilar elements in installations, taken from original art, from reproductions, from material objects, etc. The comparison with the nineteenth-century novel is worth highlighting: I take it that this assumes that it was the realist form par excellence. Building a little on this argument, I would say that if there remains any possibility for realism beyond its hitherto exhausted conventions, that possibility lies in the idea of the installation as an artefact that demonstrates the artificiality of its own narration and at the same time conserves, or better yet protects, the material reality of the objects that it exhibits or discovers.

Seventeen. Both of these issues lead to what we might call a documentary tension. Narration as a mode that requires documentary evidence in order to define itself as fiction. I'm not sure that Groys' reference to nineteenth-century novels is relevant for speaking about contemporary art. At least not for contemporary literature, which, instead of finding through its genre the convergence of all forms, proceeds through the proliferation of formats and the multiplication of different models of realism, inspired at times by elements of digital reproduction.

Underlinings, or The Era of Material Alibis

A writer pokes around in his artist friends' studios, spaces saturated with disparate objects and a certain kind of disorder, works half-finished or abandoned years ago, works that no longer seem incomplete but like shape-shifting entities in themselves. The writer wanders through these studios, in which everything seems condensed into a single moment: the moment of the first impression. The writer thinks that if there is in fact a constitutive condition of provisionality, it would be found in classifying successive synchronic snapshots of these studios.

It then occurs to the writer to compare those storehouses or rooms full of physical and tangible things with the objects that he himself uses to write. Of course, he recognizes major differences between the two classes of things (in short, the overdetermination of concrete materials and physical objects, the overabstraction of blank surfaces and writing utensils).

Another writer pokes around in his friends' personal libraries. What seems like an innocent pastime is in fact loaded with indiscretion. He has the sense that he is doing something furtive, yet he doesn't hide it from the view of the owners. In fact the opposite is true: he feels protected by the trusting vigilance to which he is subjected. The writer does not look for anything in particular, but he does hope to find something revealing. He wants to discover the physical marks of reading in books – annotations, underlinings, creased pages, schemas, any manual inscription at all – as if they were the most closely guarded secrets of his hosts. He is not seeking the unspeakable, but rather that which he believes dwells in every mark: an effort to resurrect the written word.

According to his will and desire, these marks certify the revival of the physical activity of material writing, even if they predate the so-called digital age. The marks on other people's books (other people's both because they belong to others and because they were written by others) confront him with that mixture of magic and righteousness that all restorative acts possess.

Rampant technology and a sort of individualist vocation have turned him into a kind of silent monk of immaterial writing, whose glimmers across the electronic page he perceives as the conceptual counter-point of physical writing. Sometimes he thinks of the fate of printed books, and sometimes of the vast collection of texts untethered to manuscripts; other times of the unforeseen future of a certain type of textual criticism. He thinks of those heroic writers who still believe that their texts are objects anchored in the tangible – heroic because they refuse to give up on literature written by hand. He thinks of this and of other things, until he arrives at a few examples that he designates as emblematic of the ruins and limits of the bookish culture linked to liter-ature, in large part because we are immersed in an era of material alibis.

Above all, he thinks of two things: the marks that are made on the pages of books – and the strange conceptual landscape that emerges from these modified pages – and, relatedly, of the multifarious attempts to recover the mystery, or the essence, hidden beneath that writing produced by the human hand.

Eighteen. Here I refer to writing in its capacity as an inscriptive or appropriative intervention in published books, and I propose a quotation on reading as a point of departure. In 'La causa justa', a story by Osvaldo Lamborghini, the protagonist is described in the following way: 'He did not read, but his underlinings were perfect.'[34] The character is an experienced linotypist and also an autodidact, as was typical of the profession in those days. The line compels because it is rife with ambiguities; it destabilizes our habitual notions about the act of reading and its derivative effects – for instance, what we do with what we read in a material sense. It complements the more celebrated and equally enigmatic line by the same author: 'Publish, then write.' From a certain perspective, we might even equate underlining without reading with writing after publishing.

Yet the Macedonian[35] thrust of these slogans exists in slight tension with the practical and conceptual procedures that derive from them. In reality, 'Publish, then write' refers to the literary performances that Lamborghini carried out later in life, during which he would select a book, change the title, and put his name on it. Henceforth, the book was both already published and also his own. He would subsequently write in between

34   Osvaldo Lamborghini, *Novelas y cuentos*, Buenos Aires: Sudamericana, 2003, p. 193.

35   [Translator's footnote: The reference here is to writer and philosopher Macedonio Fernández (1874-1952). A crucial figure of the early twentieth-century Argentine avant-garde, Macedonio was also a family friend of the Borgeses and a mentor to the young Jorge Luis. His irreverent readings of the Western philosophical and literary traditions had a decisive effect on the generation of Argentine writers associated with the literary magazine *Sur*, including Borges, Adolfo Bioy Casares, and Silvina and Victoria Ocampo. Portions of his magnum opus, *Museum of Eterna's Novel (The First Good Novel)* (Open Letter, 2010), were published piecemeal during his lifetime, but the final version of the novel did not appear until 1967, more than forty years after Macedonio began to write it. In subsequent decades, the novel became synonymous in Argentina with literary experimentalism, both for the unusual circumstances of its publication history and for its systematic assault on novelistic conventions (it contains, for instance, more than fifty prologues).]

the lines of the printed pages, or draw or paste figures on them. In this sense, he composed the work after it was 'published'.

The other quotation is less playful and less overtly programmatic. 'He didn't read, but his underlinings were perfect' alludes to the ideological context of the sixties, the decade that essentially defined Lamborghini and his work. During this period, the underlining of a book was not only a strategy of extracting symbolic value and constructing a secondary textual hierarchy, but also, and above all, a means of translating a more or less impartial sequence of sentences and paragraphs into a system (or a market) of urgent and transmissible ideological and political codes. By underlining one sought to fix a meaning, and thus propose a putatively correct reading, against the backdrop of a contingent universe in which an infinite number of underlinings were hypothetically possible. It is this performative function that the line invokes when referring to the idea of perfection.

And it is also this function that is invoked in a subsequent section of the story itself (also titled 'La causa justa'), when one of the characters demands, under threat of punishment, that someone else fulfil a promise simply because that promise has been articulated. The character, a guardian of the literal who is foreign and speaks imperfectly, implacably *underscores* what others say even when he is incapable of understanding the nuances of their oral language. It could even be said that because he speaks poorly and neglects the particular codes of colloquial expression, he sets himself up as the most authentic guardian of the correspondence between word and act among the speakers – in the same way that the person who doesn't read would be the best person to evaluate 'perfect' underlinings. This is because the perfect underlining, which is always subjective and therefore unquantifiable, is neither the most illuminating nor the most accurate, but rather the most inspired.

Underlining assaults the logic of reading, which is to say, the balanced progression of the line, and thus it hijacks the writing of the other, whoever the author may be. To take it one step further, underlining generates a discursive ellipsis precisely by borrowing a text produced by someone else. One might say: underlining is writing by other means.

I'm interested in the tentative principle that under-lining is a form of mediation – and not always a successful one – between the subject and knowledge; in other words, an inspired selection mechanism that does not require proof of coherence or fit, a tool that is somewhere between ruthlessly conceptual and subjectively literary. Underlining is evidently a gesture of appropriation – or better still: a private, embryonic, and personal act of appropriation, though as such, as we know, it can easily become an aesthetic or literary act if certain conditions are given in the field of art more generally.

But I also think it's worth reflecting on marginalia – that is, all those markings we make with a pencil or pen on a book, from annotations to signs – as operations that, in a way that is often overlooked, restore a practice of writing by hand from which the book is fatally detached. Detached because the book as textual form, perhaps from its very inception, required a sequential format, and because it moved further and further away from the handwritten as it became a marketable product.

Underlining and writing by hand, two practices that get scarcer every day. The old pictorial vibration present in original manuscripts finds through ordinary under-linings in books an unexpected and ironic afterlife.

Nineteen. Let me mention a few telling examples of the multifaceted symbiosis between book and annotation – or better yet, between the book and the new original, if we are to take Lamborghini's appropriative slogan literally. A volume based on Borges' annotations, *Borges, libros y lecturas*, can serve as a properly bookish, or even library-based, guide.[36] In the main branch of the Argentine National Library, in Buenos Aires, a number of books that Borges read and annotated during his time as director of the library were thoroughly examined.

Over the course of many years, textual fragments from the books annotated by Borges were collated and classified; the volume reproduces both the fragments and Borges' annotations, accompanied by lengthy explications by the volume's editors. This new book achieves paradoxical results. In the first place, it is organized around Borges' annotations, even though, as textual commentaries, these annotations occupy a secondary – one might even say belated – place in the textual hierarchy of each annotated book.

This inversion of priorities has an unanticipated effect, since it suppresses the meaning of Borges' annotations for any reader who is not deeply versed in the topics described in the texts themselves and who does not share the same set of critical assumptions as the editors. The destabilizing and interpellative force that is inherent in every annotation and that, through the modality of writing by hand, replicates the text with a difference, is silenced here by the normalizing effort to create a uniform body of text in the book format. One could add that the most obvious graphic element of the new book, the disappearance of any mark that is truly produced by a human hand, also leads to a misleading

36   Laura Rosato and Germán Álvarez (eds.), *Borges, libros y lecturas*, Buenos Aires: Biblioteca Nacional, 2010.

effect, since it is precisely the handwritten inscription made by the reader that symbolically 'rescues' a particular copy of a book from the seriality of the format itself.

In what we might define as the opposite pole of this practice (where the underlining is anonymous, or more properly speaking, undetermined), we have a work by Ezequiel Alemian, really almost a pamphlet, which consists of random pages from a book by Paul Feyerabend with handwritten marginalia.[37] Some of the pages, which are not presented in numerical order, have only a single underscore, others only two. Some underlinings are longer than others, but they're never particularly long. These are the typical underlinings of readers who are trying to isolate a strand of thought or a definitive phrase.

Readers can choose to read the context of the underlinings, which is to say, the entire page in which each one is inscribed. Alternatively, if they have neither the time nor the inclination, they can also read only what is underlined. They can also link the underlined phrases together and read them sequentially, bracketing out the large portions of the text that are not underlined. Finally, they can decide to pay more attention to what is not underlined than to what is.

In this way, Alemian's work presents itself as a compendium of various reading methods as well as of modes of reading the book itself. Are we reading a reading? Or are we witnessing the dramatization of a non-reading? The work proposes a specific procedure based on the copy and the underlining, and therefore, as often happens with these kinds of procedure-based books, we don't necessarily have to have read them to know what they're doing. Or to put it in another way, the

37   Ezequiel Alemian, *El tratado contra el método de Paul Feyerabend*, Buenos Aires: Spiral Jetty, 2010.

work expresses itself through its form. Is this the realization of Lamborghini's perfect underlining, where what is underscored has not always been read?

I offer the example of Alemian's work to highlight, or better yet, to propose, the ubiquity of the aura, which can manifest itself in a textbook, the photocopies of the textbook that contains the underlinings, and the underlinings that attempt to fix meaning through a sort of synthesis, as if they were seeking to isolate certain paragraphs in order to make those paragraphs seem like extrapolations from an unknown source.

There is a belief in this work that it is important – perhaps even necessary – to create a new text by modifying another text. But that other is not the original. The author (and who is the author: the person who made the photocopies? The person who underscored the words and phrases? The person who gathered the pages together?) does not attempt to elevate some phrases over others through the use of Feyerabend's treatise, nor do they attempt a rewriting of this particular translated version.

I have the feeling that to a large extent the point of the project is to produce aura through the use of serial objects, to create an original that is at the same time an intervention in the work of another. That intervention, though physical, nevertheless takes on the attributes of immaterial writing. The traces of that manipulation introduce – though we could also say reinstate – the auratic dimension, but on the condition that this manipulation be sufficiently evasive so as not to reveal its intentions.[38]

---

38   Charlie Feiling, who was, among other things, one of Argentina's most notable and intelligent literary iconoclasts, developed during his university years a consummate love for photocopies in general and for photocopies of books more specifically. He'd bind them with thick rings or save them in second-hand envelopes; mountains of papers

Ezequiel Alemian, two pages from *Tratado contra el método de Paul Feyerabend*, Buenos Aires: Spiral Jetty, 2010.

Nevertheless, not every individual mark on a printed surface is a guarantee of immaterial resonance. In Ricardo Piglia's *The Way Out*, we witness an annotative practice that is so mechanical and 'sophisticated' that it drastically reduces the plasticity inherent in the procedure.[39] The book includes the image of a page from Joseph Conrad's novel *The Secret Agent*, which has been marked up by the character Ida. The markings are varied and of different kinds, which leads us to believe that there is a textual hierarchy: every category of information is organized in a specific way. Emilio Renzi, who describes Ida by saying: 'She wasn't the type of person who would underline just anything', finds in the markings the definitive evidence that she has discovered a terrorist in her midst. Reading allows him to unlock the enigma, and the textual markings are the proof. At the same time, these signs, encrypted in coded language when Renzi encounters them, are the vehicles for the transmission of the deciphered message.

---

that he would place at the ends of his bookshelves so the shelves wouldn't buckle. Many of the titles he photocopied could not be accessed any other way. Feiling had a particular soft spot for cheap photocopies of poor quality, especially those whose imprint would fade with the passage of time due to the poor quality or insufficient toner used to print them. These deficient and precarious techniques imbued these book facsimiles with a nobility that the originals – which is to say, the printed books – were entirely lacking. The blurry photocopy was a better fit for the vulnerable nature of the hierarchy of knowledge, though its ephemeral character was in fact a tribute to the arduous and unstable work of reproducing that knowledge. It was as if Feiling wished to say: all erudition that is worth acquiring must derive from common materials and imperilled techniques. The greater part of C.E. Feiling's oeuvre is contained in three books: *Los cuatro elementos*, Buenos Aires: Norma, 2007 (four novels, one of them incomplete); *Con toda intención*, Buenos Aires: Sudamericana, 2007 (essays and articles); and *Amor a Roma*, Buenos Aires: Sudamericana, 1995 (poems).
39   Ricardo Piglia, *The Way Out*, trans. Robert Croll, New York: Restless Books, 2020.

lada (como si ella se hubiera sobresaltado al leerlas o hubiera estado subrayando en un inquieto vagón de un tren de la New Jersey Transit).

these institutions which must be swept away before the P.P. comes along?'

Mr Verloc said nothing. He was afraid to open his lips lest a groan should escape him.

'This is what you should try for. An attempt upon a crowned head or on a president is sensational enough in a way, but not so much as it used to be. It has entered into the general conception of the existence of all chiefs of state. It's almost conventional – especially since so many presidents have been assassinated. Now let us take an outrage upon – say, a church. Horrible enough at first sight, no doubt, and yet not so effective as a person of an ordinary mind might think. No matter how revolutionary and anarchist in inception, there would be fools enough to give such an outrage the character of a religious manifestation. And that would detract from the especial alarming significance we wish to give to the act. A murderous attempt on a restaurant or a theatre would suffer in the same way from the suggestion of non-political passion; the exasperation of a hungry man, an act of social revenge. All this is used up; it is no longer instructive as an object lesson in revolutionary anarchism. Every newspaper has ready made phrases to explain such manifestations away. I am about to give you the philosophy of bomb throwing from my point of view; — from the point of view you pretend to have been serving for the last eleven years. I will try not to talk above your head. The sensibilities of the class you are attacking are soon blunted. Property seems to them an indestructible thing. You can't count upon their emotions either of pity or fear for very long. A bomb outrage to have any influence on public opinion now must go beyond the intention of vengeance or terrorism. It must be purely destructive. It must be that, and only that, beyond the faintest suspicion of any other object. You anarchists should make it clear that you are perfectly determined to make a clean sweep of the whole social creation. But how to get that appallingly absurd notion into the heads of the middle classes so that there should be no mistake? That's the question. By directing your blows at something outside the ordinary passions of humanity is the answer. Of course, there is art. A bomb in the National Gallery would make some noise. But it

35

Luego, más adelante, otra vez el mismo subrayado hacía ver la teoría que sostenía la acción directa; no había que proponer una futura sociedad perfecta,

228

Twenty. The basic point is that textual markings and annotations reveal more than just a grammar of reading. Why in some cases do markings, and by extension all handwritten inscriptions, prolong the presence or spirit of the person who made them – even when we don't know who they were or what they meant to say – and in other cases do not? I think part of the explanation can be found in the degree of redundancy that the text attributes to the markings. In Alemian's text, the uniformity of the under-linings conceals whatever reading they might conceivably represent, and through this concealment they become ambiguous tools of a hypothetical expression. This gesture of approximation, and therefore of destabilization, gains potency through the linear simplicity of the handwritten stroke. On the other hand, in Piglia's text, the inclusion of the marked-up page within a detective narrative, with all of its critical, ideological, and generic associations, evacuates the markings of any potential ramifications outside of those that the text itself designates.

In 2014, also in the Buenos Aires branch of the National Library, there was an exhibit by Esteban Feune entitled 'Leídos'. Feune interviewed ninety-nine Argentine writers and photographed markings or marginalia in the books they possessed in their personal libraries. One of the explicit intentions of the project is to capture:

> ...that which does not leave visible or corporeal marks: the reading itself. To that end, and in order to rescue these testimonies from oblivion or from the secret romance between reader and book, bookshelf and library, I selected all different kinds of writers. Young and old, poets and novelists, famous and little-known...[40]

40 Esteban Feune de Colombi, 'Leídos. Fotografías de libros intervenidos por 99 escritores', Biblioteca Nacional, Sal Juan L. Ortiz,

Feune's project is as archaeological as it is restorative. He looks for the material traces of an operation, reading, that does not have its own system of verification, and in tracking this operation, he encounters a variegated terrain. Not only annotations in pencil or ink, but also every other sign of use, of wear and tear, of the multi-faceted engagements we all have with books.

In searching for an object as evasive and intangible as reading itself, Feune reveals, through photographic evidence, a secret economy that functions through an inverted logic: the markings rescue the book, as a physical object, from its inert condition, at the same time that they condemn it to the most definitive of declines. In each case, the markings unleash a cascade of effects, for instance (as the images suggest) on the work of Proust or of Marina Tsvetaeva.

The 'overuse' depicted in these images takes aim at the single copy, the book, the novel, the author, and literature in general. As Feune's exhibit clearly demon-strates, the book is a kind of Russian doll not only because of the chain of letters and words that compose it, but also for what it encloses and what it incorpo-rates from outside. And because, thanks to its strangely two-dimensional nature, it is capable of admitting additional meanings or values on almost the same plane as the writing itself.

Twenty-one. I would also like to examine two other illuminating examples, both of which speak to the current debates surrounding the aesthetic (and in some instances editorial) practices regarding originals and annotations. Several years ago, a group of key figures in the world of

Buenos Aires, July-August 2014.

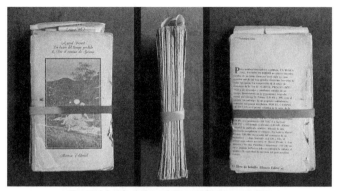

Daniel Link, Marcel Proust's *Swann's Way*

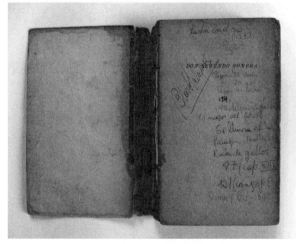

Beatriz Sarlo, Ricardo Güiraldes's *Don Segundo Sombra*

literary publishing proposed a convergence between the secret life of the marginal comment and the massively hyped publishing event. The occasion was the release of *The Original of Laura*, by Vladimir Nabokov.[41] The book's intrigue resided in the fact that each reader (in reality, the owner of each copy of the book) would possess replicas

41 Vladimir Nabokov, *The Original of Laura*, New York: Knopf, 2008.

of the notecards on which the author wrote his final novel.

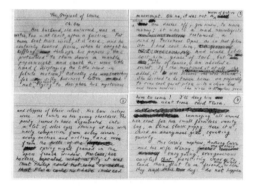

Vladimir Nabokov, four detached notecards alongside the first page from *The Original of Laura*, with the void left behind after the first notecard was detached. New York: Knopf, 2008.

These were not images of the notecards, but rather exact reproductions of the cards themselves, printed on thick material and then embedded in the pages of the book. By pressing or cutting along the dotted lines, the reader could remove the notecards and thus obtain 'specimens' that were similar to the originals.

My sense is that, in auratic terms, the result was terrible precisely because of the insistence on the analogue nature of the cards and the sheer vanity of the technique used for the simulation. On each page, beneath the rectangle that corresponded to each card, that card's text was reproduced. The reconstruction effort, which took for granted the idea that the original's material resonance would persist, was blocked by this text, which simultaneously converted the notecards, once separated from the page, into something like souvenirs from a museum. The book that remained suffered from gaping rectangular holes, which could have been used as a secret jewellery box and reminded one of a sarcophagus. One might say: that sarcophagus represents the burial ceremony of the printed book, which demands that literature disappear with it, long before the book has actually perished. One opened to any page and saw Nabokov's synthetic text beneath the hole. The mute opening often seemed much more eloquent than the cards that had so brazenly filled it.

The other example comes from the work of William Kentridge, a long-time installation artist and author of animated drawings, whose book, *No, It Is*, dramatizes the process by which the book as object gives way to the book as a material support for figurative art.[42]

---

42 William Kentridge, *No, It Is*, Johannesburg: Fourthwall Books, 2012. A more recent book by the same artist, with the same conceptual framework, radicalizes the ideas present in the earlier volume (as the title itself indicates): *2nd Hand Reading*, Johannesburg: Fourthwall Books, 2014.

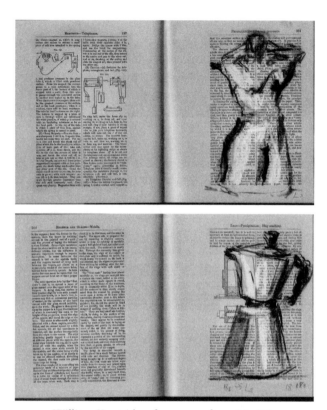

William Kentridge, four pages from *No, It Is*.
Johannesburg: Fourthwall Books, 2013.

The series of figures that he inscribes on the pages of books belonging to genres that suppress the presence of the author (old dictionaries and manuals, dated reference books that have acquired documentary value because they are no longer of practical use), should not only be interpreted as appropriations of the ideas or arguments of other artists' works. They are also reconfigurations of the visual plane neutralized by the passage of time and of the geometric conventions of reference book columns.

I would therefore hazard that these images are emblematic of a superlative kind of annotation, which differs from Lamborghini's 'publish, then write' in terms of the distinct aesthetic regimes that motivate their practice, but whose products, as combinatory objects, share the same diagnosis of the exhaustion of serial writing. Both seek to abolish the printed word as the activity most representative of writing itself.

Returning to the work of García Vega and Alemian, the question of the aura emerges through their use of what we might call verbal installations. Though different from one another, both appeal to extremely narrow verbal operations at the fringes of discursivity itself. As if they wished to say that the representation of the auratic under the aesthetic conditions of the digital world can only be produced through subtraction and displacement. On the one hand we have the displacement of Brecht, which makes the consciousness of artificiality the mechanism that allows for full confidence in the enunciative capacity of the work; on the other we have subtraction, which is to say, negativity, the silence that serves to represent the ample borders of the unsaid.

Twenty-two. I would like to return to a point about original manuscripts and their recirculation through digital printing measures. On occasion, the symbolic prestige of the manuscript has led to recovery projects that, by means of luxury editions that rely on traditional book formatting and adhere to standard academic protocols, tend to obscure the ambivalence inscribed within the original manuscripts themselves. A recent example of this is a small-format book by Susan Howe, *Spontaneous Particulars*, which uses scanned images of prestigious literary manuscripts as the basis for an essayistic reflection on archives.[43]

---

43   Susan Howe, *Spontaneous Particulars: The Telepathy of Archives*, New York: New Directions, 2014.

The outcome is a strange and at times moving collage of facsimile manuscripts, rendered in different fonts that imitate the originals, and accompanied by a solemn and measured argument about what are presumed to be the deepest questions about literature. Howe navigates through epochs and writers, identifying points of connection in order to support her own claims, which often rely solely on the path of the author herself through restricted archival collections. As if great literature could only remain relevant if it came to us in the most iconic manifestations of its original manuscript form. As if writing by hand were a sufficient guarantee that this literature could withstand the test of time.

A different hypothesis could also be put into play: that digital technology has in fact saved high literature, at a time when the very idea of high literature has come under assault. To the extent that handwritten work, in all of its forms, has become a natural preserve for digital technology, both industry and the academy have seen an opportunity to revitalize (in this case through the reproduction of originals) the symbolic value of works that are already sanctioned by these very institutions.[44]

Books like Howe's also come close to approaching the subgenre of the museum catalogue. Thanks to the power of digital reproduction, catalogues can now function simply as collections of impeccably reproduced originals. Nevertheless, due to their sometimes obscene sumptuousness, these catalogues immediately vitiate the physical resonance of the object that they intend to replicate and whose auratic effect they seek to produce. Such is the case for the relatively recent edition of the

44 This kind of literary reanimation through the digital recovery of manuscripts also reveals the extent to which technology introduces even more levels of mediation between authors and readers, contrary to the initial hope that the digital age would lead to a destruction of textual hierarchies.

haphazardly produced originals of Emily Dickinson. The most striking effect of this large-format book is the contrast between the scraps of papers and ends of envelopes that Dickinson used to write these pieces, and the extremely high quality of the reproduction and printing.[45]

In the cases of the books of Dickinson, Howe, and others, it's clear that the development of accessible techniques for the reproduction of original manuscripts has led to the appearance of new forms of textual verisimilitude linked to the facsimile. The cost of this is the exacerbation of the already tense relationship between the material substrate – which is naturally threatened by its physical precarity – and the attempt to sacralise that same material pictorially in order to justify its commercial distribution.[46]

Twenty-three. Generally speaking, manuscripts are silent in the face of these sacralization efforts. Nevertheless, it's important to recall that even though manuscripts are symbolic receptacles for expressive and aesthetic content, their principle attribute is the relationship they establish to the experience of writing. For obvious reasons, given its historical validity for aesthetic practices such as literature and painting, we still tend to associate the mark-making of the pen or pencil with the individual

---

45   Emily Dickinson, *The Gorgeous Nothings*, ed. Christine Burgin, New York: New Directions, 2013.

46   The framework for this operation is best summarized by N. Katherine Hayle's observation that, given the incorporation of digital technology into the printing process itself, the printed version should be described as one iteration of a digital format rather than a different format itself. For an analysis of Hayles's argument, see Craig Epplin's *Late Book Culture in Argentina*, New York: Bloomsbury Academic, 2014.

act of creation. But the development of reproduction techniques changed all of this, not only in terms of how we perceive and conceive of art, but also in terms of how it is constituted as an object of representation.

An example of the movement between the manuscript as an empty aesthetic form and the manuscript as the symbolic goal of the technologies of reproduction can be found in the fascinating works of Fernando Bryce. Through a series of exercises that he dubs 'mimetic analysis', Bryce reproduces – i.e. copies by hand – twentieth-century newspapers and other printed documents, primarily from his home country of Peru.

Fernando Bryce, detail from the series *Posguerra Perú*, 2013 (left).
Ink on paper, 105 drawings of various dimensions

The works that result from this operation are disquieting, insofar as they force the viewer to reconcile the seriality proper to technical reproduction with the protocols of calligraphic art or pictorial draftsmanship. In this case, the original is a serial product – recalling

Fernando Bryce, detail from the series *Die Welt*, 2008. Ink on paper, 95 drawings of various dimensions.

the appropriationist aesthetic of Warhol – and the copy exhibits the attributes of aesthetic inspiration, relying as it does on minute hand-crafted details. To my mind, this operation evokes the idea of restoring a lost asset that writing has relinquished to the technological apparatus and no longer possesses itself. These works perform a kind of contemporizing of the historical document – or perhaps even of history itself – through an artistic series, one that systematically purges its object of representation of all of its technological elements.

When I saw Bryce's exhibition at the MALBA museum in Buenos Aires a few years back,[47] I first thought of an exaggerated premise that seemed to undergird his project (and also the spatial organization of that exhibit). This copying practice could be expanded exponentially, such that the artist would eventually reproduce every single newspaper or poster related to major political events in Peru and perhaps even in the rest of the world. My second thought was of the extreme realism of the project, which aims to replicate the complex and hierarchical discursive regime of newspapers and political posters.

That complexity, however, remained below the surface; the purging that Bryce carried out was clear from the very simplicity of the work that was required to imitate the front pages of those newspapers. That is because Bryce had not inscribed those characters and figures with a view to further graphic reproduction – as, for instance, Joaquín Torres García had done when he decided to publish several of his texts in handwritten versions – but rather as a means of creating an original that would be absolutely dependent on and subservient to the mechanically produced version.

47 Fernando Bryce, 'Dibujando la historia moderna', exhibition in the Museo de Arte Latinoamericano de Buenos Aires, 29 June - 20 August, 2012.

Twenty-four. We find a different kind of restitution in the work of Mirtha Dermisache (1940-2012). Unlike Bryce, Demisache deploys a form of asemic writing. A written narrative that cannot be read – not because it derives from an unknown alphabet, but because it doesn't belong to any alphabet. She also uses newspaper formats to reinstate a scriptive presence, though she does so by purging all temporal markers and highlighting an element that, while never foregrounded, nevertheless creates the horizon of meaning for the newspaper itself: the physical layout of the page. Through their silence, Dermisache's graphic works signal a radical recovery of that which all writing hides: its profound illegibility.

Mirtha Dermisache, *Newsletter*, 1999.

My sense is that these two exercises (Bryce's and Dermisache's) do not only speak to the field of the visual arts and the art world more generally. Rather, they force us to recognize, through other forms and by other means, just how much narration has distanced itself from the activity of writing by hand. They don't simply restore this activity; they reflect solipsistically upon a connection that no longer holds.[48]

Dermisache's asemic lines also seem to allude to literary manuscripts, and what they 'say' about manuscripts through their suggestive silence is that the handwritten marks of an author always gesture toward various levels of expressivity and signification. Perhaps the semantic disposition of writing actually works against the affective possibilities of compositions written by hand; and in this sense, Dermische's asemic writing attempts to show the liberatory potential of writing once it is no longer reduced to its role as the bearer of meaning.[49]

Twenty-five. Torres García is at the centre of all of this. The dichotomy between writing by hand and seriality that Dermisache resolved with her indeterminate flourishes of the line and her playful use of standardized graphic design appears in Torres García in a less radical but more forceful way. Insofar as his aesthetic doctrine rejects perspective and all manner of realist sympathies, the individual mark becomes for Torres García the defining characteristic of the artist's aesthetic sensibility.[50] Moreover, his plastic,

48   It would also be possible to mention various works by León Ferrari (1920-2013) in this connection, particularly his 1976 piece *Escritura*. However, he also has many others works that do not fit the parameters of what I'm exploring, likely because of his tendency to synthesize or combine artistic languages, which often led to highly codified representations of both writing and the visual arts.

49   The list of critical pieces and commentaries on Mirtha Dermisache's work is extensive, especially following Barthes' observations on her work. On asemic literature more generally, one can consult a blog curated by Michael Jacobson. The blog's subtitle indicates its aims and orientation: 'This weblog explores asemic writing in relation to post-literature culture' (www.thenewpostliterate.blogspot.com.es).

50   In a 1934 conference, Torres García indicated: 'Handwriting

plane-oriented, and transcendental art often veers toward practices that are constitutive of writing by hand. I'm not simply referring to the prevalence of the line or the allegorical use of symbols in his work, but also the grids that typically underlie his constructive paintings, a sort

---

analysis, which was created in order to determine the character of each person by the particular marks of his or her writing, may or may not have succeeded in that sense (…), but it is interesting in itself because it highlights a fact that merits study and that concerns us here. In the first place, we recognize that writing *translates something individual*, to the point that, through a detailed study of it, we can discover an individual's most intimate secrets – not just their psychology and behaviour, but also their moral and emotional state at a given moment.

Thus: we can find here the foundation of the idea that *there is an individual stroke*, whether in painting or in drawing, just as there is in writing. There is therefore also a personal style of composing, of using lines, of establishing proportions, finding certain tones, etc. There are, in other words, characteristics and values of all types, which *will manifest themselves* if we work without trying to imitate what has been done by others, but rather by giving ourselves licence to express ourselves freely in the most natural way possible. This is also to say that *everyone has something*, and that if everyone has it, it cannot be lost, and consequently, *does not need to be found*. There is no basis for the fear that often seizes the artist, either of losing his personality or of needing to find it. That would imply that one wished to find one's self, which makes no sense.' (Joaquín Torres García, *Universalismo constructivo*, Madrid: Alianza, 1984, p. 42).

A quotation from Martin Heidegger, almost exactly contemporary to Torres García's formulation, seems to share the same spirit of moral transparency and the same mistrust toward the typewriter: 'Mechanical writing deprives the hand of its rank in the realm of the written word and degrades the word to a means of communication. In addition, mechanical writing provides this "advantage", that it conceals the handwriting and thereby the character. The typewriter makes everyone look the same.' Cited by Kittler. The quotation is from *Parmenides* (1942-43), trans. Andre Schuwer and Richard Rojcewicz. Bloomington: Indiana UP, 1992, pp. 80-81.

of enunciative equalizer that makes his drawings merely one element on the pictorial plane. But his paintings are indeed paintings, even if they often contain writing. It is in some of his books that Torres García seeks to violate the primary principle of the original manuscript – that it be unique – though he does so while avoiding the mediations of serial typographic composition.

These facsimile books (*La ciudad sin nombre*, *Tradición del hombre abstracto*, among others) are drawn from a series of bound manuscripts. Many combine writings with drawings or sketches that depict the places or environments where events take place. The graphic elements are not consigned to the margins or to designated panels. There is a negotiation between word and image that becomes increasingly visible as the text progresses.

The idea of a manuscript facsimile implies the survival and proliferation of the original. Torres García likely was drawn to the poetic possibilities of a mode that bordered on the artist's book. It required him to balance his desire to continue writing endlessly with the geometric restrictions of the page, a space that evidently led him to experiment with different visual registers. However, Torres García's initial intention was not to publish these texts as such, but rather to produce a large enough quantity of handwritten manuscripts to remove the typographical process entirely.

At the same time, the typography that Torres García carried out by hand (the printed letter, or rather his imitation of it), almost immediately reveals the conceptual gap between the physical and the textual original. By producing this kind of book in this way, although he clearly opts to preserve the material reverberations of the handwritten, he also ironically appeals to the objectifying quality of serial objects, which is almost always associated with printed materials.

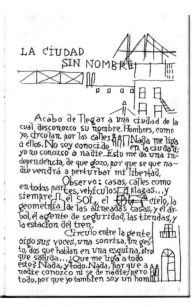

Joaquín Torres García, two manuscript pages from
La ciudad sin nombre, 1941.

Así lo quiere esa ley, que es base de la vida; lo más opuesto es lo eternamente inseparable. Y así, en el cuadro social, hay, junto a los que están en la ley, los que la contradicen; y junto, así, a cada cosa, su opuesta. Y sería tarea interminable nombrar tal número de cosas y nosotros. Pero, para entendernos ahora —digamos que, al campo social, lo divide en dos una línea, y que agrupa a sus lados, y sin que jamás se confundan los individuos que agrupa, dos clases de hombres, únicas, y aun que parezca que hay más: la de los hombres serios, y la de los pobres gatos. Y para ilustrar esto, voy a poner unos ejemplos. Sería un pobre gato, Homero, que fue un bohemio empedernido y que andaba divirtiendo a los otros en los banquetes, y que jamás tuvo un real; y Sócrates y Cristo, el primero un vago perturbador, y el segundo un hombre que ni casa tenía, y no menos perturbador, sino aun más que el otro; y que hicieron bien de eliminarles, pero bien de los pueblos que debiera socorrerles. Pero lo que hubo, fue que dejaron mala simiente y aun se sufre en el mundo por ellos. Y pobre gato fue Beethoven, borracho y sucio, sujeto hosco y poco sociable; y lo mismo Miguel Ángel, enfermo de seis enfermedades, y que, con su serio, mal arcebólico trato mayor tristeza al mundo. Y así, a miles de miles. Y de estos, desgraciadamente, se conserva la memoria (y aun tiene trazas de perdurar por los siglos) mientras que de los otros, de los hombres serios, nada se sabe, de manera, que solo puede suponerse que existieron. Y si alguno se salvó del olvido, fue por que de él escribió algún pobre gato. Pues bien: esos dos bandos se han declarado guerra a muerte, y se desprecian mutuamente; claro está que los hombres serios, con razón. Y en tales dos bandos, hay hombres empleados u ocupados en toda suerte de actividades, y por esto también en las artes. Y de estos solo quiero ocuparme. Y así, hay artistas serios, y otros que no lo son. Y los serios, si son pintores o escultores, son a los que, los asesores del estado (que ya son la cosa más seria que hay) los confían retratos también de hombres serios; ó de los otros, que, tras unos años, o unos siglos, nasarr (y no se sabe por que) también al bando de la sensatez. Tal, por ejemplo, al Greco, con razón tenido por loco en su tiempo (y con esto, Felipe II demostró ser hombre a quien

In a certain sense, it's as if Torres García had created his own private font, based on his own handwriting and design materials, but modelled after the process of serialized printing. One finds in these pages a double imitation: Torres García's handwriting mimics the printed word, while the printed word itself – or what is designed here to look like stencilled letters and signs – takes on the quality of individual style. This dual operation also recalls another, one that is absent from the scene of the page though clearly informing the entire process: the striking of a die on a surface, whose effect is to stamp a letter with ink. Did Torres García mean to suggest in this way that writing is fundamentally the material act of making words, rather than the translation of thought through the movement of the hand?

A Return to the Manuscript

Twenty-six. Any account of the current state of writing is bound to be more or less atemporal. To the extent that the written surrounds us at all moments and in different ways, there is always a substance that reactivates upon contact – even if that contact is visual – and awakens the memory or the reflex of a distant, older practice. This means that writing, as a permanent feature of our world, might best be described as a concert of similar practices with similar protocols and codes: while the results may vary slightly, these practices always retain a family resemblance.

Earlier, I mentioned the influence that Kafka's stories had on me and the feelings that seemed to emanate from them. This was the source of my desire to assimilate their radiance through sessions of what I might call empathetic writing. But the story would be incomplete if I didn't refer to another aspect of it, one that, though separate, speaks to the same thing – as if it were situated in a parallel universe or a second world, where its actions had an effect not on the act of writing but on the act of reading.

More or less during the same period when I was copying Kafka's stories, the magazine *Crisis* began to publish excerpts from an author unknown to me at the time, Enrique Wernicke. The excerpts were selected from Wernicke's diaries, which remain unpublished to this day, aside from the fragments that appeared in the magazine in 1975. These fragments were edited by Jorge Asís, whose prefatory note was accompanied by a few group photos and facsimile reproductions of the manuscript.[51]

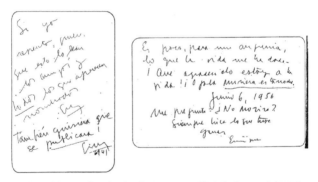

Enrique Wernicke, facsimile images of 'Melpómene' (EW's diary) published in *Crisis* 29, Buenos Aires, Sept 1975.

Due to the surprise of the unexpected, the intrigue of the mysterious, and the material effect of his greater physical and linguistic proximity, Wernicke seemed to me a more concrete hero than Kafka. We could say, avoiding the word 'dramatic': more urgent and less hyperbolic.

51   Jorge Asís, '"Melpómene." Extractos del diario de Enrique Wernicke', in *Crisis* n. 29, Buenos Aires, 1975, pp. 28-35.

Suddenly, he became the fractured and therefore total writer whose presence wasn't registered only in abstractions and parables; he spoke directly about, and from, the conditions of his life. Moreover, he had obstinately holed himself up in his wooded riverside house, at the mercy of the voracious river, whose wildness and autonomy seemed to find expression in his jittery, retiring script.

Wernicke's hand did not exhibit the firm mark of measured and speculative development, but rather the immediacy of a nervous record of his private world – a truth difficult to specify, but deeply felt. In those excerpts several of his works were mentioned (*La ribera*, *El agua*, theatre pieces, stories) alongside comments on the vicissitudes of the writing and publication processes. What was most clear was that for this author the diary served as a vehicle for things unmentionable by other means, because every aspect of his private and public life – literature, politics, love, and work – entailed an ethical dilemma that did not demand a solution but rather an inscription on paper.

On the other hand, I think it was only because of those handwritten phrases – printed on the heavy, rough paper that made each issue of *Crisis* seem like a slice of contemporary history[52] – that I succumbed to the powerful influence of Wernicke's novels. Fewer than ten years had passed since his death, despite the fact that his writing seemed to belong to a distant time and a faraway order of experience. Of course, the earliest entries were in fact from a different time, so it was natural for them to feel that way; but all the entries, including the most

---

52   On the cover of the magazine, the title appeared at the end of a phrase that served as the criterion for reading each issue and reality as a whole: 'ideas, literature, and art in *crisis*'. The magazine often avoided capitalization, and thus submitted the usual ideological hierarchies to a consistent and welcome process of equivalization.

recent ones, registered the uncertain, marginal, and provisional state in which they'd been written. Still, it was the handwritten marks that served as the real and, as it were, emotional guarantee of these phrases, and as such rendered the entire series of entries – all of which, regardless of when they had been written, referred to a past negated to a certain extent – completely contemporary. The urgent script of Wernicke was an assurance of truth as solid as the material support of any other kind of writing, albeit truthful in a different way.

Only later did I realize how strange it was that the literature of one author (in my case, Kafka) could lead to the desire to reconstitute the author himself, or better yet to grant his printed text a handwritten equivalent, and how Wernicke's handwriting led me to admire his novels even before reading them – and after having read them, to appreciate them in a way only possible for those things that are dear to us. The proximity of the tortuous diary fragments to the insistent presence of the written word created a tone. One might even say: it was the tone that Wernicke consistently believed was absent in his works.

He ultimately became convinced of the uselessness of what he had written, and of his own responsibility for the failure that the end of his life portended. Several times he mentions private writing or typewriting as the last intimate domain, and he enacts the diary as a secret and posthumous rhetorical bastion. He acted like those sinners redeemed by the very fire in which they burn, from which – either desperate or repentant – they deign to ask forgiveness. The written word is also capable of waiting for the next opportunity to appear and to continue to reveal itself by and for itself. In this way, through the chance encounters of my readings, I found myself witnessing one such scene of writerly absolution. We will probably never know what Wernicke truly felt, but to be able to perceive in that moment the materiality of his writing allowed me to intuit what writing evokes in every one of its features: the near absolute abandonment to *how* – rather than to *what* – one is writing.

Twenty-seven. Once outside the store I stopped to look at the display window. The small vase had lost its companion. The street remained empty, though it now seemed energized by my new plan – which in the long run, as we've seen, turned out to be naïve. I had found the best instrument, which has served me in part as a talisman and in part as my standard (as I mentioned at the beginning). It didn't matter what I wrote, or at least it didn't matter much. The important thing was the stage delimited by the green notebook, something like a theatre prop whose effectiveness is defined by its tameness.

I'm not exaggerating when I say that, thanks to its inexhaustible radiance, I wrote whole sections of my novels; whole novels, though I didn't put a single line of them in its yellow pages. The notebook is something like a stationary pet, one that has survived everything its owner has done. Not unlike the endless reserves of love provided by an animal, the notebook, loyal and silent, has granted me something that is priceless to an artist: more than a moral resource, an ideological compass, or an aesthetic mission, it put within my reach an empirical trick, a vital lie. Like those doors that only open when, depressed from the waiting and faced with the most gruesome destiny, our protagonist realizes that it doesn't make any sense to keep knocking.

Right now I see the notebook on the table, a short distance from the computer on which I'm writing. Due to the chance positioning of objects, it is half hidden beneath a brochure for cable channels. The brochure is several years old; it appeared some time ago tucked inside a book. It consists of an elongated sheet, folded at various points to create the appearance of columns, which list close to a thousand channels to which one can subscribe. By now, there are probably more than a thousand. Even under all of that weight, the notebook continues to silently advertise its hospitable disposition.

Writing only shows itself fully when it's read. That is the moment when it says something more than, or different from, that which it signals. It's the paradox that everyone who writes knows well: when we express our thought, it changes. I'm not referring to language in general, but rather, as I've tried to describe, the specific conditions that obtain for all writing, whether material or immaterial.

I know that this may seem like a vague conclusion. But I'm not sure that one should always be conclusive, especially when we turn our attention to those strange emanations that survive the moment of writing and point to something that is beyond the analogy of the word.

★ ★ ★

Acknowledgments

I owe a debt of gratitude to Jessica Aliaga Lavrijsen, Craig Epplin, Víctor Gomollón, Reinaldo Laddaga, Sebastián Martínez Daniell, Mercedes Roffé and – as always – Graciela Montaldo. With their presence, comments, and feedback – in different ways and through different means – they aided the writing of this book on writing.

TRANSLATOR'S AFTERWORD

Sergio Chejfec's *Forgotten Manuscript* is a difficult work to classify, straddling as it does the genres of autobiography and theory, scholarly monograph and ruminative essay, diagnosis of the digital and homage to the vanishing arts of manuscript culture. It is a slim volume of big ideas whose subtle shifts in thought often surprise the reader from paragraph to paragraph, sometimes mid-sentence. Many of *Forgotten Manuscript*'s closest literary kin will be familiar to an English-language readership and are indeed cited or otherwise referenced in the text. Walter Benjamin's essay on the technologies of mechanical reproduction. Roland Barthes's writings on *écriture* and the visual arts. The entirety of Jorge Luis Borges' corpus. Anglophone readers might also be reminded of more recent works by Chris Kraus, Ben Lerner, and Maggie Nelson, each of whom pursues, in her or his own way, an eclectic blend of personal reflection, cultural analysis, and art criticism. What these authors share with Chejfec is a restless nonconformity with the boundaries of literary genre that leads them to a search for the source of aesthetic value in the modern world. In this sense, and in line with this tradition, Chejfec's *Forgotten Manuscript* returns us to several of the most urgent questions of the twentieth-century avant-garde. What is literature? What is art? How do the changes in our technical capacity to produce them alter their function and meaning?

To fully appreciate Chejfec's approach to such questions, however, we must look beyond these international touchstone texts. For *Forgotten Manuscripts* is not only a meditation on artistic modernity around the globe; it is also an incisive reading of the Argentine literary canon of the past hundred years. Without a doubt, many of the book's major topics can be traced back to Borges: the unstable relationship between original and copy; the limits of individualistic models of literary authorship; the necessity of artifice to artistic production. But as Chejfec establishes throughout *Forgotten Manuscript*, Borges' conclusions on these topics have long since diffused into a kind of cultural common sense in Argentina, such that the name Borges (and the appellative 'Borgesian') evokes not just the oeuvre of one individual but also a vast network of family resemblances. Nearly all of the Argentine writers and visual artists discussed in these pages – from Osvaldo Lamborghini, Juan José Saer and Ricardo Piglia to Mirtha Dermisache and Fabio Kacero – belong to a post-Borgesian tradition that has extended their precursor's insights about literature to a wide range of aesthetic (and non-aesthetic) activities. The choice of this corpus is not incidental. Chejfec's arguments in the book presuppose a vision of contemporary culture in which the most serious and demanding artists are the ones who continue to interrogate our basic orientation toward words, images, and things. It is worth mentioning here that the split between writers and academics that remains the norm in the Anglo-American world has never been as stark in Argentina or elsewhere in Latin America. The feedback loop between post-structural theory and literature – for instance, in contemporary writers reading Foucault reading Borges – has been an integral feature of Argentine culture for many decades. At a moment when critics in the United States have begun to speak of a 'post-theory' generation that seeks to combine literary and academic concerns, *Forgotten Manuscript* gives us the perspective of a practicing novelist who never fully inhabited either side of that split.

A few practical observations on this translation. *Forgotten Manuscript* reproduces numerous images of artworks, manuscripts, book covers, and printed pages. Since Chejfec's comments on those images frequently address the inseparable effect of their visual and linguistic qualities, the decision has been made to retain images containing Spanish phrases as they appeared in the original version. In cases where the meaning of a Spanish phrase embedded in an image seems crucial to Chejfec's interpretation of that image, I have translated the phrase into English in the body of the text. Finally, perhaps the most important keyword in the original Spanish version of the book, *manuscrito*, has no precise equivalent in contemporary English usage. Whereas in English we typically use 'manuscript' to refer to an unpublished document in any form – handwritten, typed, or electronic – the Spanish cognate preserves its etymological connections to the Latin root, designating quite literally that which has been written (*scripto*) by hand (*manus*). Chejfec's tripartite division in the book among the handwritten (*manuscrito*), the printed (*impreso*), and the digital (*digital*) alludes not only to a difference in literary modes but also, and perhaps more fundamentally, to a difference in the systems of writing that predominate in different historical periods. That the digital ultimately relies on the handwritten, as all writing systems must rely on the systems that precede them, is a central claim of this book. At the sentence level, however, it has occasionally been necessary to highlight this difference by the use of phrases, such as 'handwritten manuscript', that may strike some readers as redundant. I have tried to limit these formulations to moments in which Chejfec underscores both the literary and the manual nature of the document in question, but perhaps the double emphasis is fitting. After all, the fate of literature's relationship to the hand – its strokes, its styles, its hesitations – is one of *Forgotten Manuscript*'s essential themes.

Jeffrey Lawrence

CHARCO **A** PRESS

Director & Editor: Carolina Orloff
Director: Samuel McDowell

www.charcopress.com

Forgotten Manuscript was published on
90gsm Munken Premium Cream paper.

The text was designed using Bembo 11.5 and ITC Galliard.

Printed in March 2023 by TJ Books
Padstow, Cornwall, PL28 8RW using responsibly
sourced paper and environmentally-friendly adhesive.